Evangelism
Through the
Sunday School

A Journey of FAITH

BOBBY H. WELCH

LifeWay Press
Nashville, Tennessee

ISBN 0-7673-3496-5

Dewey Decimal Classification: 269

Subject Heading: EVANGELISTIC WORK

Printed in the United States of America

The Sunday School Board

of the Southern Baptist Convention

127 Ninth Avenue, North

Nashville, Tennessee 37234

CONTENTS

Cover image & inside images of paper cut-out persons
Masterfile: Boden/Ledingham

Inside images of man looking at moon
Masterfile: Andrew Judd

DEDICATION

To the Members of First Baptist Church, Daytona Beach, Florida, who over the last 23 years have never questioned but have always given of themselves in attempting to win and disciple their world in their lifetime; through whom FAITH was formed. In gratitude for your willingness to allow your pastor time away to help and encourage other churches in their efforts to do the same.

To the Staff and Spouses of First Baptist, Daytona Beach, who have continued to establish the highest standards of commitment in order to lead our church's people to maximize their lives for Christ's glory.

To the Individuals from Sunday School classes who came one by one with trembling hands and anxious hearts, willing to try to learn how to win and disciple their world in their lifetime. To the hundreds and thousands who followed … learned … and taught others the same.

And especially to you, dear reader, who now has the opportunity to do the same.

INTRODUCING
BOBBY WELCH

I vividly remember the day in 1982 when I met with Bobby Welch at First Baptist Church, Daytona Beach, Florida. He wanted me to become the minister of evangelism. I recall asking him, "Brother Bobby, if I come, what will your participation be in the evangelism training?

He said, "Let me answer you this way. Whoever enrolls in the training here will have to get in line behind me. Not only that, but I will be in every STEP of training. Also, I expect every staff member and spouse to be in every STEP of the training. Does that answer your question?"

After thirty sixteen-week STEPs of training he has been true to his word. Brother Bobby is, I believe, the classic example of a pastor participator in equipping the church to become soul winners. For 15 years he has faithfully taught our level 1 class of first-time trainees. In addition to this, he personally has trained a team each STEP.

I used to imagine what it would be like to direct an evangelism training program with the full participation of the pastor. Now I know. Without the pastor, a church will never reach its maximum potential in winning souls to Christ.

First Baptist Church of Daytona Beach is greatly blessed to have this dedicated and gifted man of God to be their pastor. I am greatly blessed to have had the privilege of serving with him for 15 wonderful years.

Doug Williams

July 1997

The FAITH materials that place evangelism at the heart of Sunday School ministry is a revolutionary approach that recaptures the birthright of Sunday School, which is evangelism. It has been developed by The Sunday School Board with the full cooperation and endorsement of the North American Mission Board, and I believe it will enable Southern Baptists to baptize one million individuals in one year within the next five years. Incredible, you say. It is absolutely incredible, and God is going to bless every church that will provide this approach to Sunday School ministry.

James T. Draper, Jr.,
President, The Sunday School Board

Once in every generation, the Kingdom of God comes to a point in time which calls every believer to a lifetime opportunity. The Great Commission is the foundation of the church, and every believer is called to give his or her life in sacrifice, commitment, and effort to its fulfillment. This book is an incredible story of how the Lord has allowed the pastor and people of one church to fulfill the Great Commission in a unique way. What you will read tells how ordinary believers seized the opportunity of a lifetime to apply basic principles of Christian living to their lives. Read this book prayerfully, and you will be captured by its message and motivated to do the same.

Gene Mims,
Vice-President for Church Growth Group

December 19, 1996

Dear Pastor and Church,

About this time 10 years ago, a single twice-divorced, 30-year-old woman walked the aisle (all the way from the balcony) to stand in public confession of her commitment to Jesus Christ. That woman was me.

The Sunday before, I sat through your sermon with Cindy and Tom Robinson, Sunday School members who had become my friends and had witnessed to me. I was half mad because they had told you my life's story and crying uncontrollably because you were preaching directly to me and my need. I was convinced that Cindy had conspired with you to plan the sermon—it was that close to home.

Even though I was a college graduate with a promising CPA career, I found myself contemplating suicide the week before. I was so desperate and frustrated with trying to figure out how to live in this world.

Obviously, things have changed much in those intervening 10 years. As you know, I met and married Michael and have a wonderful family. Then, just six months ago, a whirlwind picked me and my family up and moved us on to Minnesota—land of snow, ice, and great beauty. It was hard to leave and move so far away from the only Christian family I have ever known. But, I now know that I was ready. I have grown up in the Lord, and it is going to be okay.

There's a family here too. They love the Lord and are focused on bringing lost people to Him. Every aspect of every ministry has evangelism at its core. I learned from my first family church that this is the key to an alive church that has the heartbeat of Christ. You taught me that.

In the rush of the last 10 years, and of our hasty departure, so many words went unspoken between us and our Christian family.

Thank you for equipping Michael and me.

Thank you for welcoming one so wounded and giving me time and room to heal. Thank you for pointing me to the Healer, Jesus. Thanks for letting me try to express my gifts in so many ways and for not abandoning me when I failed. Thanks for not remembering who I had been so that I could be free to become more of what the Lord wanted me to be.

Your church family is the haven where I was saved, baptized, married, and where I dedicated our youngest child, Matthew. What a great work has been done in my life there!

I am so grateful for the last 10 years, grateful for all the love and prayers, teaching, encouraging, and preaching. I am so grateful for you, Pastor and church, for speaking the words the Lord gave you, for asking the hard questions, for standing in the gap no matter what, and for equipping Michael and me for our future for Jesus and His church—wherever He leads us.

God bless you, your family, and our church family back home. We miss you!

In Him,

Sandee

Sandee

A Person,
Not a Program

FAITH Sunday School
Evangelism Ministry

IS A KINGDOM APPROACH WITH GLOBAL

IMPACT THAT BEGINS WITH ONE

SOLITARY PERSON FROM A SUNDAY SCHOOL

CLASS IN ANY LOCAL CONGREGATION.

IT IS SO SIMPLE!

This ministry process approach begins with A PERSON, NOT A PROGRAM. The origination point is not asking "what kind of PROGRAM do we need to carry out Christ's Great Commission in order to win and disciple our world in our lifetime?" No, this ministry originates at the point of asking "what kind of PERSON did Christ develop as a follower to carry out His Great Commission."

THE MINISTRY GOAL OF THIS APPROACH

1. **Build a Great Person**. That means a Great Commission person. No Christian can be a great Christian unless he or she is carrying out the Great Commission as a way of life. People may do many things extraordinarily well for the Lord, but unless they are effectively doing evangelism, they are giving their life to "unfinished business." This ministry will begin with a saved person who may have little or no commitment but is willing to try. It will take a person who may never have prayed aloud and develop that person into a Great Commission Christian who can go down the street or all the way around the world effectively living the Christ life in a way that wins and disciples others. That is what is meant by a Great Commission Christian. As you read this book, you will meet a few of the multiplied hundreds of such souls out of First Baptist Church, Daytona Beach, Florida. Such people are in all of our churches waiting to be equipped and to lead as Great Commission Christians!

2. **Build a Great Church**. That means a Great Commission Church. Just as Christians are not great Christians unless they are carrying out the Great Commission, neither is a church. When the people of a church become Great Commission Christians, the result is a Great Commission Church.

3. **Carry Out the Great Commission**. This is the inevitable result of a group of Great Commission Christians who form a Great Commission Church and live their Christlike lives. The result is that Christ's Great Commission is carried out. Therefore, this ministry approach begins with the individual person, is always centered upon individual persons, and ends with individual persons. This approach is the same as Christ's life and ministry to, and through, those early followers in order for them to win and disciple their world in their lifetime.

This same glorious adventure awaits each individual person. This FAITH Sunday School evangelism ministry is the process described above that develops a Great Commission Christian, a Great

Commission Church, and carries out the Great Commission. This ONE ministry process and system is similar to one puzzle with several pieces. The pieces are all interwoven, interlocked, and connected.

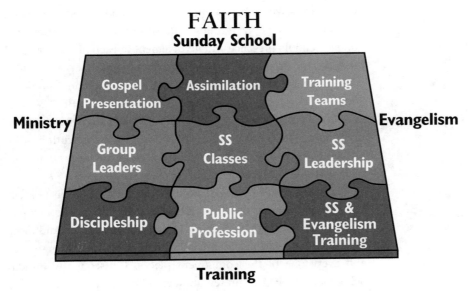

In puzzle no. 1, imagine that all pieces are covered with faces because this ministry is person-centered. These component pieces, however, all have names and are critically connected to form the ONE ministry process as in the puzzle below.

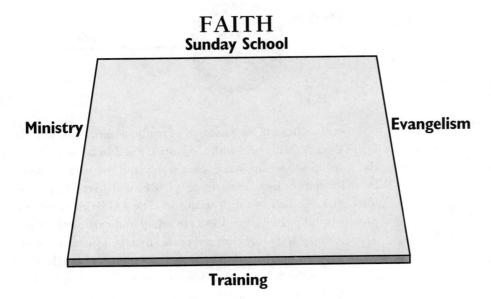

"SUNDAY SCHOOL, THE WAY IT SHOULD BE!"

When you look behind each of the connected component pieces, you will clearly see each, and all are not only attached to each other but are vitally connected to the Sunday School class. All of this begins and ends with a person and a Sunday School class. This book and the related clinic training will specifically demonstrate the Sunday School's presence and involvement in each of every facet of this ministry approach.

You will correctly conclude that this entire approach should be entitled "SUNDAY SCHOOL, THE WAY IT SHOULD BE!" Yet, this ministry has come to be called FAITH. Remember, whenever you hear about FAITH or see FAITH in action, you are in truth hearing or seeing about ONE ministry with several critical pieces that is actually "SUNDAY SCHOOL, THE WAY IT SHOULD BE!"

The name FAITH emerged from the GOSPEL PRESENTATION based upon the acronym of FAITH. This is the Training Track upon which persons travel in their equipping journey to win and disciple their world in their lifetime. This Training Track goes to each and every one of the component pieces. Consequently, Sunday School and the FAITH presentation are like two golden chains that string together the component pieces of this ministry process.

EQUIPPING AND EXPANDING THE CORE

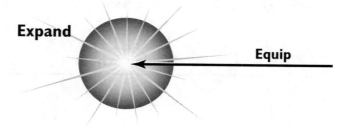

Most churches will have a variety of methods, ministries, and efforts to touch their world with the gospel. The Sunday School and the worship service are what some would call the core, or base. From the core, or base, come the people who will drive all other efforts of the church to touch its world. The FAITH ministry approach is uniquely designed to both equip and expand the core. Those coming from this core can drive any type of ministry with predicted focus and results. The old quotation, "The light that shines the farthest shines the brightest at home" could be adapted to read, ". . . shines the brightest at the core, or base."

PART 1

What Is FAITH?

FAITH GOES

TO THE DRIVING FORCE

OF THE CHURCH

WITH DYNAMIC CHANGES

People Are Open

Three things stand out in my mind as most meaningful about our Sunday School evangelism training. First, I learned the joy and discovered the power that comes from having prayer partners. Second, I was amazed at how many people are truly ignorant of the gospel. Having been in church all my life, I discovered how naive I was concerning the world. Third, I saw how open people are to the gospel when it is presented.

I had never been bold in sharing for fear of being thought a "fanatic." During these 16 weeks of training, the Lord impressed upon me to share what I had learned with two of my unsaved friends. To my amazement, instead of considering me a "fanatic," they both were open to, and appreciative of, all I had to share with them. My greatest joy in the 16 weeks was seeing one of these friends make her profession of faith.

DEBBIE RATLIFF

MEDIAN ADULT 3
SUNDAY SCHOOL
CLASS

SMALL BUSINESS
OWNER

HEART FAILURE KILLING CHURCHES

It had all the makings of a scene right out of a true-to-life hospital drama. The group of specialists, some of the best in their field in all the world, had assembled in the conference room. After a few brief comments, the lights dimmed and the screen before them became the focal point.

Viewing and reviewing such charts was nothing new for those people because that's how they usually determined diagnosis, prescribed treatment, developed new approaches, and even produced life-giving helps. They were not prepared for what was about to happen on the screen in front of them nor what was about to happen inside of them. No one in that room that day would ever forget the experience about to occur.

The screen became completely blue, and then it became a graph. Across the blue background graph came five different colored lines. Nothing really had to be said, for everyone in the meeting could see the painful, ultimate conclusion graphically demonstrated. There was a silent lull after the lines had settled into their unchanging places. Then, the leader of the assembled team, unable to hold back any longer, began to weep and sob aloud. Others fell under the same heartbreak and also wept. There were low, painful groans mingled among those other sounds. Then, the exclamation came, "This has to change; it cannot go on this way. Something must be done!"

Not medical doctors of some hospital staff but the leaders of the Baptist Sunday School Board's Church Growth Group were the people in that conference room meeting. They were reviewing the following graph.

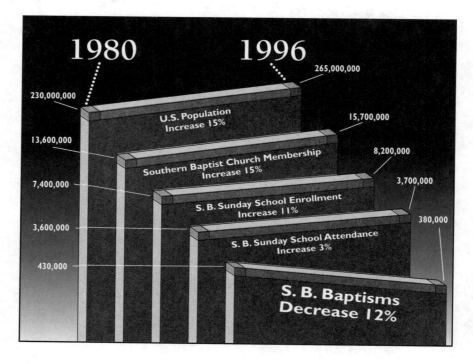

Evangelism Through the Sunday School: A Journey of FAITH

Their hearts broke at the same conclusion that surely will break the heart of any Christian who takes Christ's Great Commission seriously and is concerned for a lost and dying world.

As America's population soars, the heart of our churches' work, on an average, has "flat lined" for the past 16 years. Not two or five years, not a decade, but 16 years of Sunday School enrollment, Sunday School attendance, and church baptisms have stayed level. Look again at the line for Sunday School attendance. Look again at the line for baptisms. Those are FLAT lines indicating no movement whatsoever in our churches, on the average, for 16 years.

When a person is connected to a heart monitoring machine in a hospital and the line that reflects their heart's condition "flat lines," two things always are certain to follow. (1) That organism and person is declared DEAD. (2) Arrangements are made for the burial.

We hear of churches doing better than the graph indicates, but those usually are put before us with the hope to inspire all of us to do better. Thank God for those churches, but they do not reflect an accurate picture of where most of us and our churches really are in Sunday School enrollment, attendance, and baptisms. The graph does. Of course, Sunday School attendance and baptisms are not all that happens in our churches, but they have always been the primary indicators of church health. When those areas of ministry "flat line" or begin to decline, a church's days are numbered, usually without exception.

It may seem strange to see some areas of our church and denominational life appearing to do well even though our heart has "flat lined." Such should not create false hope. (The truth of that graph is painfully obvious.) It is likely the situation is explained because these churches are similar to a patient whose heart has stopped but certain mechanisms are introduced to keep the body going, with some activity in its system but no change to the life-giving heart. The heart must be revived if the organism is ever to function for the purpose for which God created it.

That statement is true for our churches. God created the body of Christians and called the church to glorify Himself and to win, baptize, and disciple the people of the world. That is our call, our commission, and our very HEART! Right now, our heart is "flat lined"!

God bless those people in that conference room whose hearts were broken over such tragic truth and who stood to exclaim that

The heart must be revived if the organism is ever to function for the purpose for which God created it.

"something must be done!" Thank the Lord Jesus for people with that kind of heart serving in a place to help Christian churches. In fact, FAITH would not be available to us now had it not been for that concern for souls.

You are the doctor in this analogy. FAITH is the instrument that is especially designed to not only revive and restart a church's heart work but to keep it going into the future with full health to be what God called and commissioned the church to be.

Consider what those two bottom flat lines in the graph say about all the ideas, attempts, and approaches that have been offered and tried over the past 16 years. The lines have stayed flat, so all those things we tried across the entire Convention did not help, or it took all of what was done to keep the average flat and not let it decline.

It well may be that for the most part all we have been doing in the past is just repainting the race car, changing its number, and giving it a new name but doing nothing to improve its ability to win more. FAITH is a powerful engine change! FAITH goes to the driving force of the church with dynamic changes that have been refined and tested successfully on the local church field over a number of years.

The answer to a question about other evangelistic approaches was, "FAITH is the best and only plan for now and the foreseeable future to lead Sunday Schools and churches to win the world."

The questions to us are, "Isn't our church ready for what FAITH can do, and if we don't use FAITH, will we use something out of the past 16 years of our 'flat-lined' past?" How much longer can we stay in the race by continuing to do nothing but repaint our vehicle? Write below a sentence of what you will do to help move your church beyond the flat lines of Sunday School attendance and baptism, and win the lost in your world in your lifetime.

_____

_____

_____

Does your plan offer a better organized, tested, equipped, motivated, promoted, focused, or fresher approach than FAITH? If not, this is the best time to put FAITH in the heart of your Sunday

School and church and rejoice in the thrill of a revived and restarted congregation.

PURPOSE OF THIS BOOK

To MOTIVATE the readers and their churches

To EXPERIENCE personally and collectively

An EXPLOSION in

GROWTH individually and churchwide

By COMBINING Sunday School and evangelism

Through FAITH,

an approach developed over 12 years.

The FAITH Sunday School evangelism ministry, or just FAITH for short, refers to an entire approach, system, and process that incorporate several components as a result of combining Sunday School and evangelism in a local church. In particular, FAITH is the word upon which an acronym is based. That acronym on FAITH is the outline for the gospel presentation. Consequently, the entire ministry with all of its components, was given the name FAITH.

When we first started out at First Baptist Church, Daytona Beach, Florida, 23 years ago, we did not call our efforts FAITH. As you'll read, we moved from those early efforts to the developed program known as Evangelism Explosion. After three years of experience with Evangelism Explosion, we had substantially changed that ministry to fit our Sunday School and Baptist needs. We then named the entire ministry Evangelism and Sunday School, or E/S. More and more we perfected this blending of Sunday School and evangelism, along with other needed follow-up procedures for public confession, baptism, and meaningful church membership. It became obvious that no longer would our current model of evangelism training work for us, not even our specialized, adapted version of Evangelism Explosion. That was when the name FAITH was born. I likely will always remember the day Doug Williams, Steve Cretin, and I sat in a room with three wallboards covered with the FAITH materials. One person concluded, "FAITH is the only approach that can get Southern Baptists to where we need to go for the 21st century!" We all agreed. Since that time, the approach has been enhanced to meet the needs of all churches, regardless of size.

Even though FAITH was not our original title of this ministry approach, FAITH will be the name used in this book for the sake of continuity and understanding.

THE QUESTION

"How can our Sunday School classes become more effective in evangelism, as well as in their teaching/nurturing ministry, in order to win our world in our lifetime?"

THE ANSWER

FAITH, an approach developed over 12-years, to combine Sunday School and evangelism in the most sensible way to achieve tremendous results in all areas of church growth.

THE PASTOR'S ROLE

Regrettably, Southern Baptist clergy and laypeople together baptized only 379,344 persons in 1996.

"Rise and stand up on thy feet; for I have appeared unto you for this purpose, to make thee a minister and a witness both of these things which thou hast seen, and of those things in which I will yet appear unto you" (Acts 26:16).

In Paul's testimony before Agrippa, he declared clearly that the Lord had called him as a minister to be a soul winner. Further, Paul felt that he was called to a certain group of people—Gentiles. His clear purpose was ministry that had a priority of soul-winning evangelism. Paul's call was "to open their eyes, and to turn them from darkness to light, and from the power of Satan to God, that they may receive forgiveness of sins and inheritance among them which are sanctified by faith that is in me" (Acts 26:18).

Satan wants pastors and people to do anything else but learn how to present the gospel and then extend a soul-winning invitation, whether it be in a personal conversation or from a worship service pulpit.

It was said of J. N. Barnette, former secretary of the Sunday School Department of the Baptist Sunday School Board, that he made us want to reach people, and then, he taught us how. That unbeatable combination is the ideal for each of us. My prayer is now: "Dear God in heaven, may that be said about me and every other pastor, staff person, and Sunday School leader."

One of the characteristics of an effective evangelistic church is that it is led by the pastor. That leads me to this next statement: No one can lead in the FAITH ministry like the pastor. That is expected.

I recently visited with a winsome college-age young man who has been a Christian for some time. I was encouraging him toward a church he had attended, but he voiced a negative response, "The pastor is a good preacher and all that, but he turns me off. He says how all the time that he doesn't do much witnessing or soul winning, that it is uncomfortable for him, and that he really does not know how to do it effectively." I tried to say another good word on behalf of the pastor. The insightful young Christian continued, "Pastors should witness because all Christians are told to do that. If the pastor needs help on it, he should learn how to witness and then encourage his church to do the same."

I asked, "What would you have had the pastor do?" Kindly, he added, "At the end of his sermon, I thought he would say, 'I know what I, as pastor, need to do, and I'm coming to this altar to ask God to help me. I am recommitting my life to soul winning. Who will come and join me?' Brother Bobby, if he had done that, I would have been right there beside him, joining that church and recommitting my life to soul winning." Then, the young Christian looked at me and softly asked, "Pastor, what would you do if you were he?"

If a young Christian has the spiritual insight to discern such, don't you suspect that most other Christians do? Of course they do, even though they may never mention it. They understand what the Great Commission is and means. They know what Jesus came to do and told us to do. They know who in their church should be the number-one role model and teach them how to do the number-one thing. They know. The people in a congregation are looking and listening for how and which way their pastor is leading them. That certainly includes soul-winning training and witnessing.

That young Christian's question to me is to each pastor, "Pastor, what would you do if you were he?"

This same leadership expectation is felt by the congregation toward all others on the church staff leadership team.

I've defined in these next few paragraphs the pastor's role at our church in relationship to the FAITH ministry. Those ways have emerged as the main things needed to launch the FAITH ministry and to assure its continued success over the years. I must be honest and admit that a church may have a successful FAITH ministry without doing everyone of the following things. That church will, however, never reach its potential in this Great Commission ministry if the pastor takes too many short cuts with his personal commitment or allows the church staff to do so.

Decide. The pastor must decide that the church is going to be a soul-winning, Great Commission church and then lead the church to be that in the most effective way possible. Many churches preach, talk, and applaud this philosophy of ministry but do not do it. They need to decide, and the pastor must lead them to that commitment.

To decide to be a soul-winning church does not preclude what sometimes is called a deeper life ministry. Those who know me consider me not only evangelistic but also committed to trying to lead, teach, and live the deeper life. A sample of that intention is reflected in my book, *The Sacrificed Life*.[1] The same is true with many others I know personally. There really is no conflict between being a soul-winning church and a church committed to assimilation and growth. In fact, a church that does the FAITH ministry will use what may be the most thoughtful and effective follow-up and as-similation approach there is.

A pastor and church cannot do everything that is good. Community, government, and other boards and organizations will do many things that are good and needed. Even so, no one on the face of this earth ever has or ever will attempt to win souls to Christ except saved Christians who make up the local church. Regardless of what a church does, it must do soul winning first because no one else will.

Ministry. Once the decision is made, there must be established a ministry program approach that will effectively accomplish the goal. The pastor should give leadership in this important selection. The sign at the fork in the deeply muddy ruts of an old rural road said, "Friend, be careful which ruts you choose because you'll be in them for a ways!"

It is important for the pastor to assure that the church gets into the right type of evangelism training, otherwise discouragement and default will come. Some of you—like the rest of us—have already had that experience with a variety of evangelism methods. You can identify with my pre-FAITH frustration that I have shared. You may have tried some form of evangelism training that seems to closely resemble parts of FAITH. I did too. There are many ways to do evangelism, but please hear me clearly on this, and please believe me when I say that FAITH is extraordinarily unique and different from any other evangelism approach. No matter what type of evangelism program you now have, FAITH can take you and your church farther. FAITH is significantly and singularly advanced and effective.

As I exercised my pastoral leadership in selecting this approach as our church's ongoing method, I also led our church to another conclusion about the program. That is, we would have only one "official" church program for doing evangelism. That makes it simple. No one is ever confused. There is no concern about who is doing what. We have one program, one approach, one thrust. We all train in one way, we all enlist in one way, we all go in one way, we all follow up in one way, and we all attach to Sunday School in one way. We all, staff and people, are accountable in one way. It works beautifully and productively.

The reason most of us don't get more done is because there are so many good-intentioned people running in so many different directions that effective leadership and equipping is impossible, FAITH, being the one program, will eliminate the confusion.

Support. This relates to logistical and clerical office support. It is not what pastors want to involve themselves with, but the ministry must have it. With a new program, it won't be much, but as it grows, support needs will grow. If support is not given, then the ministry soon will weaken. You'll need a room or desk space, volunteer or paid help, and budget support.

Encourager. The pastor needs to encourage the church people to be soul winners for Christ and to be a part of the ongoing training program of FAITH.

When most people come forward at an invitation, I am able to mention that a FAITH team had the joy of being in their home. I sometimes may say that several people from a Sunday School class visited them. Those are synonymous terms because we have only one visitation program. Also, those very members who visited usually will come and stand beside the decision makers, even coming down the aisle with them. If they do, I tactfully mention that to the congregation.

The people usually are reminded from the baptistry that this one person or several are being baptized as a result of FAITH and the Sunday School.

Sermons I preach will from time to time commend those who are in FAITH and give illustrations of FAITH results and the possibilities that can take place through FAITH.

I am one of the chief enlisters for FAITH. In so doing, I am encouraging the people. Almost every day of my life I meet people (especially in "counseling" sessions) who need one or more of the significant results of FAITH. I get them into FAITH. My team and I were in a home of a prospect when the wife said, "My husband is interested in learning to talk to other people about the Lord." Guess what? Yep, I invited both of them into FAITH, and soon they had joined the church and were in Sunday School and on a FAITH Team.

At the enlistment and enrollment time, prior to each 16-week STEP (one in the fall and one in the spring), I join with others and enlist new people into FAITH. I do that in a private and personal way, using the excellent materials used in FAITH. As pastor, I can do more to encourage. At the same two enlistment times, I have what we've come to call an "All on the Altar" service. I preach on Sunday morning and invite people to come and place their FAITH

Commitment Card on the altar, testifying to their intentions. This service has become an overwhelming event. I normally say, just before this invitation, "If you are a visitor, and especially if you are considering this church to be your church home and family, I'm thrilled that you are here to witness what is about to happen. What makes this church a wonderful and great church is not the pastor, staff, choir, deacons, television, or a multitude of other things. It is rather, what you are about to witness. It is the host of members who have given themselves to train and share Jesus and His victorious life. These coming will not be all because there are many, many others behind the scenes of our FAITH ministry. What an honor it is to stand among these blessed members of this church!" Then, those who filled out cards start coming. What a time, what a service, what an encouragement!

Further, time is allowed for testimonies during the enrollment phase as well as in the Sunday evening CELEBRATION SERVICE, where those who have completed the previous STEP are recognized.

There are good reasons for such attention being given to FAITH, and almost anyone in our church can point them out. (1) FAITH builds our Sunday School, which in turn builds everything else. (2) As FAITH works and Sunday School grows, all other ministries are fed and grow. (3) No other ministry has the ability to help so many members in so many important ways. (4) FAITH keeps us trained in, and focused upon, soul winning, which is the main ministry of the church.

Therefore, because FAITH feeds every other ministry in the church, it seems logical that every ministry of the church would want to feed FAITH and help it to grow and be even more effective.

Example. You can say and do all the things we've considered, but if the pastor fails to lead in FAITH by example, the ministry will never do its best. The pastor's example is the one thing he can do to lead the people and ensure FAITH a successful start and sustained effectiveness.

Pastors usually are overloaded with things to do because people feel we should lead by example. Even so, I made a deep commitment to FAITH, and for the past 15 years and 30 STEPS of training, there has never been a STEP that I have not taught a class and also had a team that I was responsible to train.

All the pastors of the Originating Trainer Churches have committed to be a teacher in a classroom of FAITH instruction. Further, each pastor has committed to be the Team Leacher of a three-person FAITH Team each STEP. The ministering staff members of these Trainer Churches have committed to model that same standard of leadership for their churches as well as those churches that will be trained at their location. God bless these good leaders because this is the example of committed leadership that will maximize FAITH among the Sunday School members and lead us all further for God's glory.

I am not the best teacher, trainer, or soul winner in our church, but all the members know that their pastor is trying to be on the front line and is not calling them to do anything that he is not trying to do himself. The pastor must lead by example, and so should all the church staff members.

That young Christian I spoke of at the beginning of this part really was asking all of us pastors that question, "Pastor, what would you do if you were he?"

BETTY SMITH

MEDIAN ADULT 5
SUNDAY SCHOOL
CLASS

HOMEMAKER

Thanks Church

Almost every week the mail brings another letter to my house announcing that I have been selected as a potential winner in a fantastic sweepstakes. Well, I feel about my Sunday School evangelism training as if I've won a fantastic sweepstakes, and I want to tell everyone about it.

All my fears and embarrassment over talking to a stranger about Jesus, seemed to fade away. There is not anything in the Christian experience to compare with the surge of joy that floods your senses as you realize that you have been brave enough to share the wonderful gospel message and a person understood and accepted and believed in Jesus Christ.

I can never thank my church enough for offering me this great ministry opportunity!

Staff Leadership

After I began my Sunday School evangelism training, I made a commitment to teach children in Sunday School. I came into the training because of the role model of the entire church staff, which shows that this is the most important ministry of the church.

HARVEY WIGGINS

4TH GRADE
SUNDAY SCHOOL
TEACHER

LAW ENFORCEMENT
OFFICER

"**We believe** that every Sunday School and church should implement as quickly as possible the FAITH ministry. We have been praying, planning, and promoting this all-out effort to equip every Sunday School to win their world in their lifetime through FAITH. The next few years of our work together are projected based upon this innovative, effective, and proven approach. We earnestly believe that FAITH is the best way to revolutionize our Sunday Schools, not just to survive, but to thrive to the glory of God in the 21st century."

Jimmy Draper

Gene Mims

Bill Taylor

FAITH IN BRIEF

...is the most effective way to both teach and reach through Sunday School.

...training and visiting is done not during Sunday School class times, but at other times through the week.

...combines an evangelism ministry with Sunday School work.

...teams visit both members and prospects of their respective class/department.

...is based upon a three-person team from a Sunday School class/department.

When you hear and think of all the other churches that use FAITH, you will know that it is the precious body of Christ in those churches actually touching individual lives and meeting individual needs through this ministry. FAITH truly is "People-to-People." The participants are busy, imperfect laypeople from all walks of life who have their own struggles. Even so, they and their churches have put first things first and have been gloriously blessed in the process.

You will discover testimonials from laypeople throughout this book. These saints of God are no different than those dear souls in your church, but these people have been trained in, and are committed to, FAITH. These accounts you'll read are but a few of hundreds we have accumulated. Their individual highlights will vary greatly, but their commonality is that all of them came out of their lay ministry through FAITH in their Sunday School class at their local church.

The goal of these testimonials is to:

(1) Assure the reader that busy laypeople can do FAITH in a splendid way.

(2) Keep focus always centered on people.

(3) Emphasize the wide range of results and blessings to be expected.

PAUL ANDREWS

MEDIAN ADULT 4
SUNDAY SCHOOL
CLASS TEACHER

SENIOR HIGH
SCHOOL
ASSISTANT
PRINCIPAL,
RETIRED

Sunday School Excited

I had just taken over as a teacher of the Median 4 Couples Class when information about FAITH Sunday School evangelism training was started. After enrolling in Sunday School evangelism training, I started recruiting members of the class to join me. Before it was over, our entire class was involved in Sunday School evangelism training in some way or another. That made our Sunday morning class twice as exciting as before. We shared our experiences, doubts about the memorization, fun, and the learning process.

As a participant, I now have a better understanding of the gospel and the reason for my existence. I have grown to admire the members of the class.

NORMA BOK

5TH AND 6TH
GRADE SUNDAY
SCHOOL
TEACHER
FINANCIAL
SECRETARY

Twenty-Two Years

I know it was the Holy Spirit working in my life and beginning a new work not only in Norma Bok, but her family as well.

I had several obstacles in my way when I signed up for the Sunday School evangelism training. But, I just couldn't seem to back away from the commitment I had made, so I began my first semester of Sunday School evangelism training.

To say that Sunday School evangelism training changed my life is an understatement! As a result of Sunday School evangelism training, I found what I had been lacking—a personal relationship with Jesus Christ. As if my eyes had been opened for the first time in over 20 years as a Christian, Sunday School evangelism training helped me to see that there were hurting people in the world and in my family who needed the wonderful gift of eternal life, and I had to do what I could to share it.

My husband began to ask me about our visits and even sat with my ill mother so I could attend every week. The greatest gift of all came when after 22 years of praying for my husband, he received eternal life. I am convinced that would never have happened had it not been for this wonderful program the Lord put in my life.

I started out in order to learn to share the gospel with others, but first I needed to get the "log out of my own eye." That was 10 years ago. I have remained in Sunday School evangelism training and have grown in my own life. I have been able to share the gospel with my 5th and 6th graders in Sunday School, have shared with my immediate and distant family, and have been able to train others who started out just like me, with fear and trembling.

OUR CALL TO COMMITMENT

FAITH is the commitment to combine Sunday School and evangelism with the pastor, staff, and leadership leading and equipping the laypeople of their local church to fulfill their Great Commission command in a way that produces powerful New Testament results.

In FAITH's call to commitment are nine key ingredients that should be reviewed.

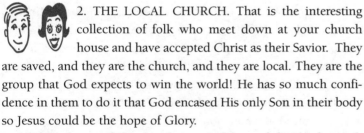 1. THE GREAT COMMISSION. There is no doubt in any evangelical church about what is meant by "The Great Commission." All know that the term is based upon Matthew 28:18-20. It means that every saved person has the command and commission from God, Jesus, and the Bible to win souls to Christ and then train them in His ways.

It has been found impossible for a local church to carry out this Great Commission and command on the scale our Lord intended without the ingredients found in OUR CALL TO COMMITMENT. We do indeed have a great God who demonstrated a great love, gave us a great Savior, and provided us a great honor by choosing us to carry out His Great Commission. All that and more compel us to put out a great effort to fulfill His great expectations. The FAITH approach enables us to mobilize people from every place within the church and every stage of Christian development into a great force to carry out the Great Commission in both reaching and teaching.

2. THE LOCAL CHURCH. That is the interesting collection of folk who meet down at your church house and have accepted Christ as their Savior. They are saved, and they are the church, and they are local. They are the group that God expects to win the world! He has so much confidence in them to do it that God encased His only Son in their body so Jesus could be the hope of Glory.

Look at the people in church next Sunday and during the week submerged in their work-a-day world. They may look unlikely, but all of them are awesome spirit beings, fully able in the power of God and the person of Jesus to snatch souls out of the jaws of hell, to put people on the road to heaven, and to direct them to a victorious life here and now. Who else do you know like that? When they become unified with Jesus and each other on the very thing that Jesus longs to do from within them, LOOK OUT! THAT'S THE

LOCAL CHURCH, IN THEIR COMMUNITY, WINNING THEIR WORLD, IN THEIR LIFETIME!

No wonder every "Tom, Dick, and Harry" with every program, scheme, and proposition that comes down the road wants to tap into the local church, right there where you attend. They recognize that there is nothing like the local church. The local church was not established for worldly gain but spiritual riches. You really are sitting on a "gold mine" at your local church! It is a gold mine not in earthly treasure but in souls to be won to the glory of God.

It is my experience and happy discovery that the local church does not have one problem that soul winning through the Sunday School will not solve. That's right, not one! If you need a person to play piano, go win one. If you need money, win souls, and they will bring it. If you need a closer walk with the Lord, go soul winning. If you are depressed, go tell people about how much God loves them. I'm sold on that conviction! I've already had almost 25 years of a growing, glowing, and blessed experience in one local church that has centered on the Great Commission. God is going to bless and help any local church that does that. There has never been a ministry approach like FAITH Sunday School evangelism ministry. It can bring a Sunday School and church congregation to a victorious place quickly.

The local church is where it must happen, and FAITH is the way to do it.

Sunday School ➡ FAITH ➡ Evangelism

3. SUNDAY SCHOOL. One of the most apparent and distinctive features of FAITH is the ongoing, intentional use of the Sunday School to accomplish evangelism. Every pastor, education director, and those concerned for evangelism know that this is not only the way it should be, it is the best way to do both of those ministries over the long haul. That was the logical reasoning why evangelism was recognized as a function of the Sunday School in the beginning.

Part 2 of this book reveals more about how these two tend to be on a collision course in churches. Tragically, evangelism always loses. Actually, many variations and models have been used trying to combine Sunday School and evangelism. Some have worked better than others, but almost all fail. The beauty of FAITH is that it is destined to work well. You'll discover why in this book. Also, the beauty of FAITH is that it completely equips participants in a multiplicity of ways and builds them into Great Commission Christians.

Churches that do make some connection of visitation with Sunday School usually note three weak points inherent to their method. One, there is no ongoing, on-the-job training that is committed to perfecting a person's ability to witness and minister. Two, most often there is one person on the church's visitation team that does the majority of the ministry. Three, as a result of the first two weak points, this type of combining fails in large part to equip believers to train others. This third point undermines the best efforts by churches who do combine Sunday School and evangelism. That is unfortunate for the church, the people, and for Kingdom work. With just a little redirection of effort and use of the FAITH ministry, those churches could be conserving valuable training efforts and amassing an awesome army in their Sunday School. Their people would be equipped. If they move away, they are trained "Sunday School evangelism missionaries" to their new church.

The points I have just mentioned are what urge me to say that regardless of what form of evangelism you or your church may be using, the FAITH approach is certain to move your church and its people to a new dimension and level of ministry.

As stated, most churches are without any combined ministry effort by the Sunday School and evangelism. The FAITH Sunday School evangelism ministry will provide those churches and Sunday Schools with the maximum results. FAITH has a call to commitment on behalf of both Sunday School and evangelism.

 4. COMMITMENT. Commitment is sadly lacking in many churches today, and sometimes the lack is within the pastor and staff. Commitment is the giving of one's self to a task, a call, a command, an assignment. Too many people are holding back too much, or they are giving too much to the wrong thing.

If the local church is going to be used of God to win its world in the 21st Century, it must be willing to pay the price. That is not measured in dollars but in measurably determined commitment, which begins with the pastor and staff. They will have to be committed to move out of a comfort zone into more focused leadership as soul-winning disciplers and in turn lead the church to follow. If your church raises the standard of commitment, you will be thrilled to see committed people join you. Otherwise, you are destined to attract uncommitted people and will find yourself surrounded by a sea of the uncommitted. The results are that all will slowly sink and drown in their lack of spirit-filled determination. Pastors, staff, and leaders should lead the charge for people to rise to a new level of commitment.

Experience shows and you will discover that in the Sunday School class and church, untold numbers are waiting to be challenged and led to new spheres of Christian living and serving. There is no doubt that they will follow as far as leaders will provide commitment to take them.

FAITH is the exact instrument, when placed into the hand and heart of a willing pastor and staff, that can move them and their entire congregation to an unparalleled level of Christian discipleship.

 5. PASTOR AND STAFF. They must lead the effort to reach your Sunday School's and church's potential with FAITH. That is, the FAITH emphasis is what every pastor should be leading members to do. The main thing is to reach the lost and the needy and in turn teach, train, and disciple them. If we are going to lead anywhere or anything, the work begins at this point! FAITH has been a major accountability factor to help me, our staff, and people to do, on a regular, ongoing basis precisely what we knew we should be doing anyway.

My personal leadership commitment to FAITH, as pastor, has been in several ways:

(A) I am a classroom teacher for the STEP 1 (Semesters of Training in Evangelism Partnership) course of training for beginners. I teach the beginner class because the pastor is able to draw in new people who otherwise might be reluctant to enroll. Especially do new people in the church like this because it gives them an opportunity to get better acquainted with the pastor.

(B) I am a Team Leader of a three-person FAITH Team. Each week, we learn together and then we go out and visit together. Then, we come in and rejoice in the victories together. This is a wonderful time not only to teach and train but to encourage and disciple while being blessed myself. There are many extra side benefits to this approach of equipping the saints. All effective leaders know the value of identity with those to be led.

(C) I lead the staff in the FAITH ministry. The staff commitment and participation is an important part of the pastor's leadership role. If the pastor has exemplified a high degree of commitment and participation, there should be no difficulty for the staff to follow with exactly the same commitment.

When Doug Williams and I first talked about this type of ministry, he asked me what would be my involvement. I told him that whoever else got into this ministry, they would have to get in line behind me and follow me. That was my commitment.

I, as the pastor, am an officer and member of the Sunday School of our church. I understand that the church's command is to reach the world for Christ. Therefore, what better place could I do more with my influence and leadership? Of course, if that is true for me, it is true for all others of our staff.

(D) All of our ministering staff are FAITH Leaders. Their job assignment is to be on a FAITH Team. All of them are leaders of a team. Each of them is a class facilitator. That gives powerful leadership to their areas of ministry throughout the church.

(E) The spouses of those on our paid ministering staff are expected to be a part of our Sunday School and evangelism ministry. Does that mean that if a ministering staff member or mate refused to be part of FAITH ministry they would be out of a job? That is correct. This is not some type of heavy-handed dictatorial demand. That expectation and its importance is explained to staff people at the beginning.

Such a call for commitment should not seem unusual. After all, these people joined our staff and are being paid to help our church accomplish the goal for which Christ established it. Since we believe that Sunday School and evangelism through the FAITH ministry is the best way our church can maximize our resources to carry out the Great Commission, it is consistent with our beliefs and expected that all staff be committed. Even those staff members who are not directly related to Sunday School understand that when the Sunday School does well and the church grows, their areas of ministry are affected in a positive way as well. These staff members are "team" members and are happy to be such a positive part of an exciting work such as FAITH.

I do not say that every church should require this of their staff and their spouses. I do say that staff people can be led to a deeper level of Christian living and service and in turn can lead others to the same.

Most churches do not have several paid staff people, so in those churches, the pastor's leadership, along with the Sunday School leadership, will be far more essential.

(F) Sunday School leaders, deacons, and other members in leadership positions are deeply impressed, blessed, and inspired by

When Doug Williams and I first talked about this type of ministry, he asked me what would be my involvement. I told him that whoever else got into this ministry, they would have to get in line behind me and follow me. That was my commitment.

such leadership commitment on behalf of their pastor, staff, and their mates. Consequently, there exists an overwhelming pull on all the people to follow this leadership example of commitment in order to do what they already feel in their hearts and what they know they and the church have been commanded to do by our Lord.

Over a period of time, such commitment is established that people are drawn to it and then lifted and strengthened by it. When we have our "All on the Altar" service twice a year, at which time we enlist new people for participation in FAITH, it is almost breathtaking to experience a mighty demonstration of commitment to Sunday School and evangelism for Jesus' sake! It is especially moving to me as I witness multiplied hundreds stream down the aisles and remember that when I started we had 18 people. That number then shrank to three people. Now we have numbered over 500. How humbling and worthwhile is the investment of a pastor, a staff, and a church to lead and train the saints! No matter what size the church is, no matter the size of the Sunday School class, no matter when or where the class or church meets, this can be the experience of every church in the world that has a Sunday School and a willing leadership—willing to try, and ready to express FAITH.

6. LEADERSHIP. Leaders are those who are willing to take the risk to help get others to where all need to be. Leaders come from everywhere and out of every background. Leaders are those who know in their heart that a certain thing needs to be accomplished, and they come to a point where they cannot wait any longer. They know in their hearts that something must be done! At that point, they take a deep breath and say, "I will try with all my heart to do it!" There always are risks involved, including the fear of failure. Leaders sometimes fail, but nevertheless, conscientious leaders do try. They lead and see victories won!

Soldiers of the lowest rank and with the least likely personalities have won the nation's highest decoration, the Medal of Honor, because in a certain moment they decided to "go for it." FAITH calls out deacons, Sunday School teachers, class members, staff, wives, youth, and others to rise to the occasion and lead where they can. Leaders in the church are not born. They are born again. They are ordinary people who are obeying God and following Jesus.

Leaders sometimes fail, but nevertheless, conscientious leaders do try. They lead and see victories won!

7. LAYPEOPLE. They are to be believed in, encouraged, led, challenged, and urged to try. That is the way to develop great saints of God.

There are saints who wait to be equipped, encouraged, and let go. Jesus is living inside of them and is yearning to do what He came to this earth to do.

Someone asked me, "Why do so many people year after year come down the aisle to commit themselves to train and visit through their Sunday School?" The answer is that they come down one at a time. One single person, one married, one teen, one senior adult. Each one comes with an anxious heart, a trembling hand, and a fear of failure, but they come willing to try. When they do try, they do what Jesus wants them to do and the Father commanded them to do. They then receive extraordinary assistance, blessings, and rewards from the Lord. That is followed by confidence and purpose. They see family, friends, and acquaintances affected by the Holy Spirit because they were trying to learn, to grow, to tell, to help, to be a blessing, and to let Jesus loose inside them to do His holy work upon a world around them. Dear Christian, all the forces of heaven are waiting for you to try so they can rush to enable you!

If you will commit yourself to this ministry of FAITH and try, you will be amazed at what can happen in your heart, your life, your home, your Sunday School class, your church, and your world!

8. EQUIPPING. Equipping is to provide people with what they need to accomplish their objective. It could be a stove for a cook, a compass for an explorer, or paper for a writer.

For Sunday School, with the responsibility not only to reach but to win the lost, FAITH is the equipment to accomplish those objectives. The good people of our Sunday Schools cannot be expected to do what they are assigned without being trained to do it. Most of them are doing a great job. Their problem is that too many of them have been given a bad job description and no equipping to function correctly. They deserve equipping.

The Sunday School Board has clearly reestablished the Sunday School's equipping ministry to do that and more. It is the FAITH SUNDAY SCHOOL EVANGELISM MINISTRY.

FAITH SUNDAY SCHOOL evangelism training is an equipping approach with dynamic impact upon people's lives, their Sunday School, their church, and the world around them.

Someone asked me, "Why do so many people year after year come down the aisle to commit themselves to train and visit through their Sunday School?" The answer is that they come down one at a time.

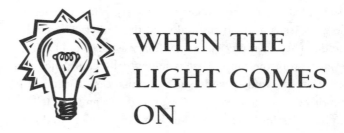

9. RESULTS. I already have indicated some of the results you can expect from FAITH. I can assure you that the results and benefits will be far beyond what you might imagine at this point. The results are presented in two formats; I will not discuss them here. You are, however, welcome to get excited right now because the results of FAITH are positive, powerful, and far reaching into the lives of you, your people, the church, and the world. Welcome to the thrilling, life-changing world of FAITH!

WHEN THE LIGHT COMES ON

"They said one to another, Did not our heart burn within us, while he talked with us by the way, and while he opened to us the scriptures?" (Luke 24:32).

FAITH is a tested and proven ministry that should be in every one of our churches and Sunday Schools because it offers the potential for our churches to explode for the glory of God and win their world in their lifetime.

More than several times pastors and their staff have said over and over again, "This is exactly what we've been waiting for!" Others said, "Our staff has been planning and praying for months in this direction. Now the Sunday School Board has it ready for us to put to use immediately."

At one of the prospective Trainer Churches visited, the pastor was almost moved to tears as he invited us to pray with him and the staff to thank God for this help to them.

A past president of our convention and one of our premier pastors said over and over, as he heard this ministry approach, "This is of God - This is of God."

Dr. Joe Brown, pastor of Hickory Grove Baptist Church in North Carolina said, "The only reason we've ever used any other evangelism method was because the Sunday School Board did not have one. Thank God that day is over - count us in!"

Two leading Florida churches called to say, "Whatever it takes we want to be in at the beginning of this approach in combining Sunday School and evangelism."

At the beginning of the FAITH presentation of the gospel one California pastor shouted, "Praise God, I know where this is going!"

A grandmother of over 70 years of age came to her daughter and said, "Honey, the other ways of learning to share the gospel were always just too hard for me, but I believe I can do FAITH and I plan to be on a Sunday School team this fall."

A pastor in Arkansas said what drew him most toward FAITH was the way it combines Sunday School with evangelism.

A pastor in Alabama felt he had only 20 minutes before he had to leave the staff meeting where the FAITH concept was being presented. After only a few minutes he said, "Wait, I can see this is not just another *program* but it is exactly the process we need. I'll be here for the next two hours in this meeting to hear more, and our church will definitely be one of the first to implement this.

Dr. Daryl Eldridge, Dean of Religious Education at Southwestern Baptist Theological Seminary observed the FAITH approach to combining Sunday School and evangelism. He commented, "I believe God is in this. You know my heart. If our churches are to succeed, our pastors and staff need to succeed. If pastors and staff are to succeed, seminaries must equip them to succeed. The seminaries can be effective partners in this Great Commission vision, and we at Southwestern Baptist Theological Seminary would like to join this venture from the very beginning.

A foreign missionary from Central America just heard about the Baptist Sunday School Board and the FAITH ministry. He called to find out if they could implement this in the next few months in their churches. He exclaimed, "This is what we must have if we are to grow these churches!"

Bill Taylor asked a room full of pastors and staff members a loaded question. "What would happen at your church if your Sunday School began to spend their time really focusing on people and their needs. And what if, in each Sunday School class, there was one or more 3-persons teams going out each week to reach people already in Sunday School as well as those not in Sunday School. What would happen?"

The room was immediately ignited with excitement and exclamations. "We'd have the biggest revival ever!" "Our building could not hold them!" "The people would grow like never before." "Our church could be what we always wanted it to be for Christ and our community!"

Yes, The Light Came On!

MARISSA DIFAZIO

SINGLE ADULT
SUNDAY SCHOOL
CLASS

MEDICAL STUDENT

Bolder Faith

So many times I prayed and asked God to use me somehow. I wanted to become stronger and especially bolder with my faith. When I heard about our Sunday School evangelism training, I realized that with the Lord's help, this was the perfect way to do these things.

Our Sunday School evangelism training has provided me with the boldness that I have longed for. It has increased my knowledge of Scripture and has taught me how to use key portions of Scripture to relay the gospel message effectively. I have so much more confidence now as I share my faith, and for that reason, I share it with much greater frequency.

Sunday School and evangelism truly is a marriage made in heaven and is just waiting to unite at your church!

Some days ago a woman told me, "Last night my senior adult mother said to me, 'Honey, you know I've always wanted to learn how to share my faith, but the materials to study were always too long and there was too much to remember.' Then my mother extended her hand toward me, palm up, and began to spell on her fingers, FAITH. She then looked at me with a smile of confidence and stated the obvious, 'Honey, I believe I can learn FAITH!'"

In that dear senior adult woman's heart, face, and hand, "The light had come on," with FAITH! It will come on in the hearts, faces, and hands of those in your church too.

A pastor called from Corpus Christi, Texas, and said, "I've just heard about FAITH. That is what our Sunday School and church needs, and I want to be in at the beginning!" Practically the same was said by the education staff at the church in Oviedo, Florida: "We've got Sunday School, and we've got evangelism, but we want them combined in the same effective way that FAITH had done it for you! Where do we get the stuff to do it?"

"It is what we have been missing! It will work!"

Any person who has the slightest understanding of (1) the requirement of the Great Commission for the local church and (2) how the Sunday School is organized and functions will always grasp and complement the FAITH approach. As the person hears how FAITH unites a church's Bible teaching organization together with the church's priority goal of evangelism, it is immediately obvious that such a union will build the Sunday School and build the evangelism ministry at the same time. Both together will join hands and hearts to carry out their church's Great Commission. At that moment the exclamation is always the same: "It is what we have been missing! It will work!"

Such reactions reflect the obvious common sense that FAITH makes for Sunday School and evangelism. Ministers of education, preschool directors, directors of Sunday School, new members, recent converts, state directors of evangelism, ministers of outreach, men, women, boys and girls, pastors, deacons—you name them—all can easily see it.

Good news! Your church's laypeople and leaders are just as alert as anyone. When they are given even the explanation of FAITH, they will give the same enthusiastic acceptance and approval. You know why? It is because they simply are acknowledging what God is up to and Jesus inside of them is saying, "Yes! Yes!" Friend, that is a winning combination for you, your church, and your city!

So, the light is coming on! You could be saying now, "Well, but I'm not sure this is what our Sunday School and church needs to do right now." But the other question is, "WHAT WILL YOU DO IF YOU DON'T?"

So, the light is coming on! You could be saying now, "Well, but I'm not sure this is what our Sunday School and church needs to do right now." But the other question is, "WHAT WILL YOU DO IF YOU DON'T?"

What are you going to do for you, your Sunday School and your church if you don't do FAITH? Is there another ministry that makes more sense? Is there one that has a better potential of building your

Sunday School and also reaching the lost? Is there one that can unite so many aspects of your church life? Is there one that will produce such capable leaders? Is there one that can so focus and galvanize a pastor, staff, and church leaders? Is there one that can touch lives and meet needs more effectively?

FAITH is a tested and proven ministry that should be in every church and Sunday School because it offers the potential for churches to explode in results for the glory of God and to win their world.

Sunday School and evangelism truly is a marriage made in heaven. FAITH is ready to unite at your church!

YOU HAVE EVERYTHING YOU NEED, RIGHT NOW, RIGHT WHERE YOU ARE!

You already have all around you just what it takes to see your church family, you, and your community move to a wonderful new dynamic of ministry and living. You don't have to move to a new church, your community does not have to become a boomtown, and a lot of other things do not have to come about that usually are associated with an explosive new dynamic outburst in a church. That is superduper good news! It's absolutely true, too, and I believe you'll agree as you think about these five items.

✅ 1. SITUATION

The situation, circumstance, and condition of our culture and society have resulted in billions of dollars of sales for burglar alarms for home and vehicles, gun sales, and the like. Drugs and all the rest, including the breakup of the American home, are heartrending. Statistics reinforce the point.

Another side to our current situation is what appears to be a large and unparalleled unrest, frustration, and even desperation among the leaders and laypeople of the churches. Pastors and staff are involved in forced terminations and personnel changes at an unprecedented rate. The people in the churches find themselves struggling to go on individually and collectively.

In the midst of these things is an interesting happening. "Religion is breaking out everywhere," said Bill Moyers, in *USA Today,* October 11, 1996, referencing The Gallup Organization's findings. Americans are indicating that the influence of religion is increasing in their lives. Attendance at religious services is up. Such heightened desire for spiritual information can be the opportunity to witness and win others to Christ.

"Public confidence in both organized religion and clergy has been renewed," said Gallup's finding, according to Moyers. My guess is that people have confidence in the stability of local congregations. People in your community are looking to your church with more confidence than before.

In my view, if you take a closer look at the situation in which we now are called to serve, it has the potential for a great awakening right in our own church and town. That is not the only thing you have going for you, right now, where you are. People and leaders want something good and godly to happen in them and around their church. There is new interest. The nation's moral need is obvious.

✅ 2. SAVED PEOPLE

The one insurmountable asset you have right now, right where you are, is saved people. Please don't just quickly move by this statement, but think about it. When people are born again, Jesus comes to live within them in the power of the Holy Spirit, according to Scripture. Jesus is the same yesterday, today, and forever, which means that Jesus is in all the saved people in your church. He has the same desire to do what He was sent to do, "to seek and to save that which was lost" (Luke 19:10). When Jesus is having His way in us, we act, talk, and walk like Jesus, and we will continually allow Him to carry out His ultimate purpose. That is the Christ life and the Spirit-filled life. Don't let people try to get you to believe that they or you are living a Spirit-filled, Christ-centered life if soul winning is not their ultimate purpose. That idea would not be consistent with God's plan, Jesus' mission, our commission, or Bible teachings.

✅ 3. SPIRIT

God has given power to enable all saved people, including those at your church and you, to get loose, to let Jesus be Jesus in, and through, them. "Ye shall receive power, after that the Holy Ghost is come upon you: and ye shall be witnesses unto me both in Jerusalem, and in all Judaea, and in Samaria, and unto the uttermost part of the earth" (Acts 1:8). "I can do all things through Christ which strengtheneth me" (Phil. 4:13).

Wow! Think about what's down there at your church right now, right where you are!

☑ 4. SUNDAY SCHOOL

While you are thinking about what's good and right at your church, thank God for your Sunday School! There is nothing in the world like the Bible Teaching-Reaching Ministry of a church. It is sad to hear of denominations that see Sunday School only for children. Sunday School is the backbone and spinal cord of a church. I have often said that if a person were forced for some reason to choose between attending worship service or Sunday School, I would tell them to go to Sunday School. I'm thankful that hardly anyone is forced to make such a choice, and I'm aware that some pastors may not feel as I do. My reason for such a statement is because there is just nothing like an organized Bible Teaching-Reaching Ministry with age-graded and properly grouped departments and classes. In a properly functioning Sunday School, you can have everything needed to build great Christians who will build great churches that will carry out Christ's Great Commission.

OK, stop and review what you have right where you are, right now.

• You have the SITUATION that is ripe for a movement of God inside and outside your church.

• You have SAVED PEOPLE who are indwelled by the Savior desiring to get loose in them to accomplish the Father's plan through them and their church.

• You have the SPIRIT OF GOD to empower you.

• You have the SUNDAY SCHOOL, which is the core of the church's structure and already is organized with the mission to reach and teach. Nothing else in a church comes close to the Sunday School in organization and human resources.

Nevertheless, you may say, "So what? We have all that right where we are, right now, but we are continuing at about the same pace we've been going for years. What makes those four things come together to do things differently?"

☑ 5. FAITH

You have the opportunity of FAITH, which has the ability to bring it all together in a comprehensive ministry approach through the Sunday School.

God has proved it over and over that when He is working His will, He can take what looks like a hopeless, empty situation and turn it into a miracle to bless multitudes and glorify Himself. All God waits for is willing people.

"She said, As the Lord thy God liveth, I have not a cake, but an handful of meal in a barrel, and little oil in a cruse: and, behold, I am gathering two sticks, that I may go in and dress it for me and my son, that we may eat it, and die. And Elijah said unto her, Fear not; go and do as thou hast said: but make me thereof a little cake first, and bring it unto me, and after make for thee and for thy son. For thus saith the Lord God of Israel, The barrel of meal shall not waste, neither shall the cruse of oil fail, until the day that the Lord sendeth rain upon the earth. And she went and did according to the saying of Elijah: and she, and he, and her house, did eat many days. And the barrel of meal wasted not, neither did the cruse of oil fail, according to the word of the Lord, which he spake by Elijah" (1 Kings 17:12-16).

"When it was evening, his disciples came to him, saying, This is a desert place, and the time is now past; send the multitude away, that they may go into the villages, and buy themselves victuals. But Jesus said unto them, They need not depart; give ye them to eat. And they said unto him, We have here but five loaves, and two fishes. He said, Bring hither to me. And he commanded the multitude to sit down on the grass, and took the five loaves, and the two fishes, and looking up to heaven, he blessed, and brake, and gave the loaves to his disciples, and the disciples to the multitude. And they did all eat, and were filled: and they took up of the fragments that remained twelve baskets full. And they that had eaten were about five thousand men, beside women and children" (Matt. 14:15-21).

God's will is for Jesus to lead His people to accomplish God's purpose in winning the world. Praise God, "You have everything you need right now, right where you are!" The Lord is waiting.

God's will is for Jesus to lead His people to accomplish God's purpose in winning the world.

DON'T SAY NO!

Some Christians and churches fail to reach their God-given design and potential because someone keeps saying no for them. It is possible for such Christians and churches to feel happy, cared for, pampered, and satisfied, but the truth is that God has much more planned for them, and they are being denied the opportunity to discover it.

As a hobby, I cultivate bonsai trees. This living art form occurs by intentionally dwarfing the plant, thus, causing otherwise normal trees to live their entire lives in a reduced condition. This results when the caretaker repeatedly says no on behalf of the living organism.

As the curator and cultivator of the trees, when they indicate that their roots, leaves, and branches desire to extend, I simply say no for them. Then I take subtle, nontraumatic action to back up my no answer on their behalf. The trees, then are slowly, surely, and painlessly denied their full potential.

One of my little trees is over 80 years of age with the natural potential of being 80 feet in height. The tree, however, is only 28 inches high and is confined to a small pot, only 5 inches deep. The growth potential is denied because someone else is saying no for the tree.

You might say, "How sad and cruel for the trees." Actually, the trees are pampered, living in beautiful, expensive containers filled with specially prepared soil, receiving measured amounts of water, with prescribed foods. So these trees actually are blessed in an unusual way.

The most tragic thing of all is that the illustration from plant life is perpetrated upon the Christian people in our churches all the time with unspeakable damage and irretrievable loss! Churches fail to reach their God-given design and potential because someone keeps saying no for them. It is possible for such Christians and churches to feel happy, cared for, pampered, and satisfied. The truth is that God has so much more planned for them, and they are being denied the opportunity to discover it.

During a break at one of our International Evangelism Training Clinics at First Baptist, Daytona Beach, Doug Williams and I were having a casual conversation with several staff members from a well-known church. They had been here as part of one of our three-person Training Teams, doing on-the-job visitation. Having experienced our laypeople's excitement, ability, and commitment, they were now exclaiming to Doug and me, "That is what we are missing back home in our church. We need laypeople with the kind of commitment we see here among these laypeople!"

Two more days of clinic training passed, and the same staff members had another conversation with us. After inquiring about our week-by-week ministry and training, they declared, "We do not believe that such a level of commitment can be called for or sustained by our busy laypeople."

Those good men did not hear what they were saying and conveying. Their people did need a deeper commitment, but the staff members were not willing to believe in those people to the extent they would issue the necessary challenge to commitment. Some staff persons and other unpaid church leaders are not willing to pay the leadership price for deeper commitment from their people since it will require at least that same commitment level from them as leaders.

Leaders must not say no for the laypeople of their fellowship. We should believe in them, give them a chance, encourage them, call on them to try, example commitment before them, and think yes on their behalf. Don't say no for them. Turn them loose, and let them go with FAITH.

CAN WE SLEEP WHEN PEOPLE DIE?

"I looked on my right hand, and beheld, but there was no man that would know me: refuge failed me; no man cared for my soul" (Ps. 142:4).

There are many things for which care is needed in this world. The children of China and the hungry of Africa truly need care. Our water and air need care and concern. Some will cry out, "We need to care for the spotted owl and the sea turtle too!" Who do you know who truly cares for the souls of men and women?

God the Father cares for souls. He gave His only begotten Son that whosoever believed in Him would not perish, but would have life everlasting. God did that because He cares for unsaved souls.

The Lord Jesus cares for souls. He died upon a cruel, humiliating cross for unsaved souls.

The Holy Spirit cares for unsaved souls. He convicts lost souls of their sin and need for the Savior.

The saved in heaven care for unsaved souls. They rejoice every time a lost soul is saved.

The lost in hell care for unsaved souls. One such doomed soul as seen in Luke 16 was begging that someone should tell his brothers not to go to hell.

The BIG question—who in your world, in your community, in your church, in your home, cares for souls? The BIG answer should be—every saved soul should care for every lost soul. It is unthinkable that a lost person in hell should care more for souls to be saved than do Christians.

A preacher and his young son were returning home after a meeting in a distant city. As they were traveling along, a car passed them

The BIG answer should be—every saved soul should care for every lost soul. It is unthinkable that a lost person in hell should care more for souls to be saved than do Christians.

on a hill. There was the squeal of tires, the crash of steel, and the sound of broken glass as an approaching car collided head on with the car that had passed the pastor and his son.

When they could no longer be of help, the pastor and his son continued homeward. The boy sat stunned, seemingly reliving the experience over and over. The screams of agony and the dying of the occupants of that car had made a tremendous impression on the boy.

The boy could not eat when they arrived home. He went to bed early. The father became concerned about his son for the boy still had not spoken. In the middle of the night, the young boy cried aloud. His father went to his aid. The father asked, "Son, can't you sleep?" The boy replied, "Daddy, when people die, how can we sleep?"

DR. DON WHITE

COLLEGE/CAREER
SUNDAY SCHOOL
TEACHER

PHYSICIAN

Healings

As a medical doctor, I have had the opportunity to encounter people with many physical and spiritual needs. As a result of having a simple and easy-to-use gospel plan presentation, I have been able to share the plan of salvation with several patients.

Just this past week, I shared with a patient in the hospital who has no hope of living, barring a miracle. Because of the Sunday School evangelism training, I was able to clearly explain to her that God is not only love, He is just. She was able to understand the plan of salvation presented. She prayed and asked Jesus to be her Savior and Lord. Now, she has a hope and ability to face her imminent death with the assurance that she will spend eternity with Jesus.

The training has equipped me and given me the confidence to share Christ's love with my patients and to offer them more than physical healing, which is only temporary, and to see them spiritually healed.

Evangelism Through the Sunday School: A Journey of FAITH

Too Busy

I had some of the best excuses yet. I work a 40-hour-a-week job, plus an additional 15 hours a week in my husband's business. I have four children at home. I had already convinced myself that Sunday School evangelism training was for people who didn't have much to do and had a lot of extra time on their hands. After all, I attend church three times a week, and there just wasn't any way I could be expected to attend another night and prepare training homework as well. After all, I have been out of school too long and have forgotten how to study and do memory work. Those good excuses surely would be enough for anyone who would approach me to enlist in the Sunday School evangelism training.

I sat through the motivational banquet and heard several people give their testimony about Sunday School evangelism training. When I heard Brother Bobby's challenge, there was a tug at my heart, so I signed the commitment card to enlist, with butterflies in my stomach!

I thought I was too busy, but I can honestly say that other than accepting Christ as my Savior, this is the greatest experience I have had as a Christian.

ROMA NEAT

MEDIAN ADULT 5
SUNDAY SCHOOL
CLASS

SERVICES
COORDINATOR
FOR BLIND
CENTER

PASTOR DENNIS
HENDRICKSON

MISSIONARY
LACEIBA,
HONDURAS

Eye Opening

Our church in an upscale area of LaCeiba has 60-70 in attendance, and our people wanted a training ministry that would equip us, reach the people around us, and grow our church. The Sunday School evangelism training ministry team from First Baptist Church, Daytona Beach, had the answer.

The response of our Sunday School people was wonderful as the team's training and examples inspired us in a way that could only be described as EXPLOSIVE! One young lady who had never even prayed out loud before returned after only two training sessions and shouted with joy, "I never knew it could be so good!"

In three nights of visitation, our five teams of three people each presented the gospel 62 times and had the joy of leading 68 people to pray and receive Christ! Now, our Sunday School teachers and others who won them are involving them in our Sunday School and church. That was an eye-opening experience to me about what laypeople could do once equipped and how fast they could learn. I praise the Lord for what this ministry has done for our church and community, and I am thrilled at the prospect for the future months and years.

---

[1]Bobby Welch, *The Sacrificed Life: Keys to Intimacy with God* (Nashville: Broadman Press, 1992).

Evangelism Through the Sunday School: A Journey of FAITH

How Can FAITH Help?

FAITH can,

in any size congregation,

bring the largest number of people

in the shortest amount of time to do the

most important work for any church—

which is to carry out our

Great Commission.

FOUR-N-ONE

For a Sunday School and church that intends not only to survive but thrive in the next century, it must have, as a primary goal, to accomplish four things in efforts to win and equip the world. FAITH will do all four of those things in one approach.

EQUIPPING **EVANGELISM**

FAITH

ACCOUNTABILITY **MINISTRY**

1. EVANGELISM must be combined with Sunday School.

2. MINISTRY to those who already are members of Sunday School in a caring and keeping way.

3. EQUIPPING the members of Sunday School to do the work of ministry as they themselves grow in Christlikeness.

4. ACCOUNTABILITY network is established in the most non-threatening way for all Sunday School members and prospects.

Undoubtedly, there are churches that do a superior job in some of these four areas. To do so most of the time requires a church to mobilize, maintain, and staff each area as a separate ministry. The vast majority of churches cannot do that unless they find a way to incorporate them. FAITH is that approach!

Before we consider the *four areas of results,* I want to make some important points.

In studying FAITH, you will go inside a dynamic new approach to Sunday School, evangelism, church work, and lay-equipping discipleship. Some people have viewed it as advanced Sunday School work. What follows in this book is not to serve as a manual for training but is to encourage you and your Sunday School to understand and implement FAITH after you have received clinic training. Beyond that, there are two concerns I have for you as you digest this book.

Danger 1.—You might say, "I don't think our church would be prepared to handle all the many positive results produced by FAITH." Don't panic. While you will immediately experience favorable results, all those results will not happen in the first year, but they will come. God knows what you can handle, and He will pace your results through FAITH.

Danger 2.—"This is too much stuff to do!" may be someone's exasperation. No, that is not true. It may seem that way at first glance, but that is not the case. In this book, I have attempted to give you a clear view of FAITH, and in doing so, I have taken the ministry apart piece by piece. Consequently, there are a number of pieces for you to examine. The positive result is that you will appreciate the detail and thoughtfulness of all its aspects, and you can understand FAITH and visualize how it will work in your Sunday School and church.

The fact is, all of the pieces pull together as if magnetized to join forces with each other. In some ways, the development is like a spiritual snowball moving, growing, and advancing. FAITH pulls the parts together in a smooth and effective way. Remember, you already have much of what is needed to make FAITH work.

WILL "FAITH" HELP ALL SIZE CHURCHES?

A recent study profiles "typical" Southern Baptist churches as "primarily small churches." Research director Phil Jones indicated:

> The "typical" Southern Baptist church has 233 total members, of whom 168 are resident members. The current pastor has been at the church three to four years. The church has 70 people in its Sunday morning worship service. It reported five baptisms and five other additions during the 1994-95 church year. It has 98 enrolled in Sunday School with 55 in attendance. ... While large, growing churches receive a great deal of attention, the Southern Baptist Convention continues to be composed primarily of small churches. Seventy percent of SBC churches have 400 or fewer members, and less than 10 percent have more than 900 members. (*Florida Baptist Witness*, Jan. 23, 1997).

Will FAITH work in every size church from the smallest to the largest? Yes!

One of the most appealing aspects of FAITH is that a smaller church, without multimember paid staff can receive all the benefits as a mega church with many paid ministers. That is possible because FAITH is completely interwoven into the Sunday School, which is at the heart of a church regardless of its size.

FAITH can, in any size congregation, bring the largest number of people in the shortest amount of time to do the most important work of any church—which is to carry out our Great Commission. That is done through the Sunday School. FAITH answers the "how" question for the pastor, leaders, and church who, in their own lifetime, earnestly want to win and disciple the world. FAITH shows them how regardless of the size of the church.

BETTYANNE
EDSON

MEDIAN ADULT 3
SUNDAY SCHOOL
CLASS

ELEMENTARY
SCHOOL TEACHER

Personal Growth

One of the reasons I decided to join First Baptist Church, Daytona Beach, was because of the Sunday School evangelism training. How I underestimated what such training would do for me! The benefits have been a vast increase in my personal Bible study time, thereby bringing me into a closer relationship with Jesus; increased prayer time, bringing me even closer to Jesus; a better knowledge of the gospel—why I believe what I do and why everyone else should; a genuine burden for lost souls; increased fellowship with other believers; and deepened friendships with fellow believers.

RESULTS YOU CAN EXPECT

Dr. Gene Mims has written a book that outlines Kingdom *principles,* and First Baptist, Daytona Beach's, evangelism experience has outlined Kingdom *practices.* In Mims' book, *Kingdom Principles for Church Growth,*[1] principles that have long been set in motion by God are highlighted. First Baptist, Daytona Beach, has been practicing a ministry approach that clearly demonstrates those great principles and has wonderfully rejoiced in the results of them.

First Baptist, Daytona Beach, had already experienced the four results that Dr. Mims wrote about in his book and clearly categorized. No doubt that has happened in many churches through the years. God has been at work!

Mims stated on page 68,

> True church growth is not the result of methods. It is the result of the supernatural activity of God, who desires to redeem persons to Himself. When a church discovers and applies the kingdom principles of church growth, increases in the church naturally follow.[1]

In his book, *"Kingdom Leadership,"* (Nashville: Convention Press, 1996), Dr. Michael Miller focuses on the kingdom leader's calling, character, and competencies. The book is a call to Christ-centered leadership, and that's what FAITH ministry is about.

I want to document and detail to some degree the Kingdom growth results that you should expect when your Sunday School and church commit to Kingdom building through FAITH. It gives almost immediate and lasting results that will be experienced in:

- Sunday School attendance increase
- Lost people being saved
- Baptisms increase
- Other additions to the church increase
- Worship attendance growth

There is more, however, much more that you can expect that will revolutionize lives and an entire congregation. Here are those broad results with a brief explanation of each.

⊘ EXCITED MEMBERS. Church members will become excited about their Great Commission growth journey.

⊘ SOUL WINNERS. One of the primary goals is to train members to be effective soul winners.

⊘ EQUIPPERS. The hope and goal is that some trained soul winners will train others to do the same.

⊘ LIFESTYLE WITNESSES. This is one of the ultimate desires for members of a Sunday School and church.

⊘ DISCIPLERS. This is a natural outcome of the training design and a FAITH Team's configuration and interaction.

✔ ATTENDANCE INCREASES IN SUNDAY SCHOOL because those people from the FAITH Teams visiting and caring have come from, and on behalf of, a Sunday School class. They visit people of their own age and interests for a particular Sunday School class and department.

✔ LOST PEOPLE GET SAVED because those visiting for their age group Sunday School class are capable of witnessing effectively and leading a person to salvation in Christ.

✔ BAPTISMS INCREASE as a result of those who pray to receive Christ in the homes and later are baptized.

✔ OTHER ADDITIONS TO THE CHURCH INCREASE by way of church letters and statements of faith in direct proportion to FAITH Team visits.

✔ WEEKLY LEADERSHIP MEETINGS become a revived, energetic rally with an atmosphere of excitement about people. The meetings form a golden link that connects Sunday School and evangelism effectively.

✔ COMMITMENT LEVELS RISE as pastor, church, and Sunday School leaders lead to a new standard of commitment.

✔ ENROLLMENT IN SUNDAY SCHOOL INCREASES because one of the emphases that is stressed in FAITH Team visits is that of "on the spot" enrollment into a Sunday School class. Special materials are used for that enrollment.

✔ NEW SUNDAY SCHOOL UNITS increase to accommodate the additional members to Sunday School and can be forecast by the number of teams visiting, per a certain age group.

✔ ORGANIZATION OF SUNDAY SCHOOL EXPANDS as a result of the increase of people, units, workers, and leaders.

✔ SUNDAY SCHOOL MEMBERS NURTURED in that the visitation assignments are structured to do ministry maintenance calls to those people already members of the Sunday School class who need a care and keeping visit.

✓ WORSHIP ATTENDANCE GROWS because of the visits being made and because of the growing Sunday School's commitment to the worship service where they see their new friends make public their decisions and some are baptized.

✓ LEADERSHIP TRAINING occurs in an ongoing way and supplies a multitude of needs. Many of our church's leaders and workers now in Sunday School were in FAITH first, where they were developed and discovered, then later enlisted in service.

✓ WORKERS FOR MINISTRY are developed and take up meaningful and rewarding ministry responsibilities. This, in turn, serves as a cause for them not to drop out but to continue on their growth and service journey.

✓ LONGEVITY OF WORKERS is extended and is more fulfilling because FAITH is focused to do both ministry and prospect visits. This eliminates the "conscience struggle" within the Sunday School worker that can arise when no provisions are made to visit both groups.

✓ THE PRAYER MINISTRY OF THE SUNDAY SCHOOL CLASS is an integral part of a successful FAITH team and calls for more prayer and yields more confidence in prayer.

✓ FRIENDSHIP/FELLOWSHIP CIRCLES are created among the FAITH Team members and the prayer ministry along with those of the Sunday School class and the evangelism class. This network is an extremely powerful care and keeping aspect to help people feel that they belong.

✓ A PEOPLE CONSCIOUSNESS becomes a superseding influence among the church people because their training, interaction, and involvement sensitized them to real personal needs of those they have met. Their lives, prayers, efforts, classes, and families center upon people and not programs. People are starving to have true friends and to have their hurts helped. This will become an inviting and appealing feature of your church to those outside it.

✓ ACCOUNTABILITY GROUPS are realized in almost every network of FAITH and should be credited for the high percentage of people continuing in the training and going on to places of leadership and service.

⊘ DISCIPLESHIP TRAINING is accomplished by those who have been equipped in previous STEPS of FAITH. That is done through group study, individual study, and on-the-job training in evangelism and ministry. Doing Great Commission work deepens discipleship.

⊘ NEW DYNAMICS TO FELLOWSHIP will be quickly appreciated as the joy, excitement, rejoicing, and expectancy of changed lives infiltrates the Sunday School, worship, and all other areas of church life. It can become almost electric in a Sunday School class as well as in a leadership meeting or a worship service.

⊘ MINISTRY INVOLVEMENT ADVANCES in both community-wide efforts and overseas endeavors as the people get a larger vision through Christ for the world.

Perhaps you are saying, "This is just too good to be true. Why, it sounds like FAITH will solve every problem and meet every need imaginable!" No, probably it would not do that much for every church, but it will come close to doing that for most churches. When the Sunday School is profoundly touched, moved, and mobilized, all those results I have detailed and even more are predictable results. Our experience at First Baptist, Daytona Beach, has declared all of them not only predictable results but proven results.

I want to give you a fuller appreciation of what you have to look forward to, and get excited about, as those results fall into the four results groups Dr. Mims underscored in his book.

FOUR AREAS OF RESULTS

 1. NUMERICAL GROWTH. "Howbeit many of them which heard the word believed; and the number of the men was about five thousand" (Acts 4:4).

Recently, I was sitting on the hillside overlooking the Sea of Galilee in Israel where Jesus spoke to multiplied thousands, and I thought, *Wow, Jesus surely could draw a crowd to tell them about the love of God.* Most of our Bible schools, books, and seminars teach us how to prepare and preach great sermons. We usually don't learn how to get many people there to hear them. People are important, all of them, crowds of them. They need to hear about and experience the love of God in Jesus. You and I need to reach all we can while we can. "The hand of the Lord was with them: and a great number believed, and turned unto the Lord" (Acts 11:21).

FAITH will increase your Sunday School and church numerically. It may be that there are some few Sunday Schools and churches that conclude, "We are growing and winning our world as quickly as we can and don't need FAITH to accelerate our numerical growth." FAITH still will appeal to such churches because of all the other benefits listed, and all churches must develop Great Commission Christians regardless of the church's size.

Our Sunday School attendance has increased in an accelerated way since we at First Baptist, Daytona Beach, combined Sunday School and evangelism. We have been able to chart our course to an average attendance in Sunday School of over 2,000 by the year 2000. FAITH has had us on this route for the past few years. It requires a net increase of 73 per year in Sunday School. We are right on schedule! Any church can chart its own course of growth but must have a way to get there. FAITH can do it!

New units for Sunday School increase in response to the actual increase in Sunday School and those projected to attend. One can actually forecast where new units are needed based upon the number of Sunday School members in FAITH in certain age groups.

Baptisms will grow because lost people will continue to be saved month after month and year after year. FAITH is not a "quick fix" that dissipates after a short surge. It is oriented for the long haul of continual consistency.

Other additions by way of letters and statements also will increase because FAITH Teams are prepared to maximize the results of every visit whether the need is for a soul-winning presentation, an encouragement to a member, or a prospect who already is a Christian.

Enrollment in Sunday School increases because FAITH Teams are equipped to do "open-on-the-spot" enrollment of a prospect into the class of the visiting team.

Worship service attendance will grow in relationship to other numerical growth! This is a hand-in-glove relationship as the worship service and the Sunday School complement each other through FAITH and both rejoice in the victories.

The list of numerical growth resulting from FAITH includes the size of your weekly leadership meeting, the number of workers enlisted in service, and the number of leaders produced.

We are right on schedule! Any church can chart its own course of growth but must have a way to get there. FAITH can do it!

2. SPIRITUAL GROWTH. "Grow in grace, and in the knowledge of our Lord and Saviour Jesus Christ. To Him be glory both now and forever. Amen" (2 Pet. 3:18).

FAITH will grow your Sunday School and church spiritually. A Great Commission church will have a deep desire not only to see lost people saved but to see saved people grow into the likeness of Jesus "Whom we preach, warning every man and teaching every man in all wisdom; that we may present every man perfect in Christ Jesus" (Col. 1:28).

What does grow in the "likeness of Jesus" mean? I am persuaded that it directs us to be about what Jesus was about with the same drive, disposition, and determination that He displayed during His earthly ministry. Jesus is the same yesterday, today, and forever (Heb. 13:8). So, whatever you saw Christ do in the yesterdays of His earthly ministry, you may be certain He wants to do that same thing in, and through, you today. You may also expect and prepare for Him to be the same tomorrow and forever through you.

Sadly, many Christians try to make the case that one must reach some predetermined level of spiritual maturity before attempting to witness to others. That is a grave error. The New Testament Christ-like example was to do both witnessing to the lost and discipling of the saved at the same time. Jesus said, "Come ye after me, and I will make you to become fishers of men" (Mark 1:17). That challenge is to go along with Jesus and be like Him, and as you do go, you will fish for souls.

That challenge is to go along with Jesus and be like Him, and as you do go, you will fish for souls.

Kim, a young lady in our church, said that while on an African mission trip, she was impressed by the sight of an American preacher and an African believer as they trekked from village to village preaching, witnessing, and helping with medical needs. Kim said that what struck her were the conversations of the men as they walked cross-country between villages. They talked and taught each other, as Christian brothers, about deeper things of the faith and Kingdom work. All the while, they were on a soul-winning expedition. As she heard and saw them, she thought, *This must have been the way it really was with Jesus and His disciples.* I agree with Kim. Jesus' model is to go soul winning and discipling along the way. This is the model and pattern you will see in FAITH.

JESUS IS THE MODEL OF FAITH

FAITH will develop many spiritual disciples and is perfect for new converts or anyone else desiring to grow in Christlikeness. Here is why:

- ⊘ you study
- ⊘ you are accountable
- ⊘ you practice
- ⊘ you keep records of your progress
- ⊘ you learn to stand and speak for Jesus
- ⊘ you learn how to pray and its importance
- ⊘ you learn to allow the Holy Spirit to lead
- ⊘ you gain confidence
- ⊘ you become part of several small groups
- ⊘ you share in others' concerns and victories
- ⊘ you get and give encouragement
- ⊘ you discover your ministry
- ⊘ your home, marriage, and work are touched
- ⊘ you do discipleship follow-up
- ⊘ you continue in the work of the Great Commission
- ⊘ your spiritual leadership emerges
- ⊘ you have opportunity to train and disciple others
- ⊘ you learn the Bible and how to use it
- ⊘ you learn to handle obstacles the devil offers.

Never Really Grew

I first heard about Sunday School evangelism training during one of Brother Bobby's sermons. The fact that 95 percent of American church members have never led anyone to Christ really hit home with me because I was one of those people. The Lord really convicted my heart and led me to enroll in the training.

I received the gift of eternal life at an early age and never really grew in the Lord as I should have. I feel that I have grown more spiritually in the past 16 weeks than I have in the past 16 years of my life.

PATTI HICKS

YOUNG ADULT I
SUNDAY SCHOOL
CLASS

HOUSEWIFE

Discipline and commitment are foundational stones for any effective lifelong journey of spiritual growth. FAITH is firmly planted upon those two things.

 3. MINISTRY GROWTH. "The Son of man came not to be ministered unto, but to minister, and to give his life a ransom for many" (Mark 10:45).

FAITH will expand ministry. As Jesus begins to have freedom and access through believers in the Sunday School and congregation to carry out His Father's desire, people will become lifestyle witnesses. They will discover all sorts of places and opportunities to touch lives, meet needs, and win their world. Their focus will be soul-winning evangelism.

People will become ministry driven. Their lives will be unwaveringly committed to the fact that (a) the most important ministry possible to any needy person is to see him or her become a saved child of the King; (b) no ministry is worthwhile if the ultimate goal is not to seek and save.

The response of Pastor Charles Roesel's First Baptist Church of Leesburg, Florida, is a case study on this subject. I encourage you to read his book, *Meeting Needs, Sharing Christ.*[2] You will be inspired by seeing Leesburg's "ministry evangelism" forever and always focused upon soul winning. Also, Dr. Richard Lee, pastor of the Rehoboth Baptist Church in Tucker, Georgia, is leading the church in finding ways to touch and win their world outside their church walls.

At First Baptist, Daytona Beach, our people's hearts truly did swell with Christ's soul-winning compassion for our city. We then were led by God to see all the needy, lost souls we were driving by every Sunday on our way to celebrate and worship at church. We had 2,000 people on First Baptist's property on any given Sunday morning, but there were 140,000 lost and unchurched people around us. We had to do something more.

We experienced a movement of God within us to win our world in our lifetime. Because of FAITH, we had been sensitized and burdened by Jesus in us. Our eyes and hearts opened wider to that world in the community around us.

At the time of that compassion crisis for our community, we made some decisions for the sake of souls beyond our church walls:

> (1) To go to those who never will come to our church.

We had 2,000 people on First Baptist's property on any given Sunday morning, but there were 140,000 lost and unchurched people around us. We had to do something more.

> (2) Not to be intimidated in the difficulty of doing follow-up or sometimes not being able to do it.
>
> (3) To organize and emphasize by way of the staff and budget to be sure that our ultimate goal clearly is that of soul winning.

Our congregation exists to glorify and fellowship with our Heavenly Father through growing in Christlikeness and sharing His plan of salvation with the lost of our world. Therefore, every ministry is to contribute toward the church's reason for existence. We made our list of ministries and headed into the city to reach more of those 140,000 we drove by each Sunday on the way to church.

4. MISSIONS ADVANCE. "How then shall they call on him in whom they have not believed? and how shall they believe in him of whom they have not heard? and how shall they hear without a preacher? And how shall they preach, except they be sent? as it is written, How beautiful are the feet of them that preach the gospel of peace, and bring glad tidings of good things!" (Rom. 10:14-15).

FAITH will advance personal involvement in overseas missions.

Christ in us, has a longing to win the lost no matter where, including those beyond our own continent. Overseas soul winning is the expected results of an ever-expanding heart for lost and needy souls.

International mission work gives persons such an infusion of confidence and boldness that they come home to do more effective work for Jesus than ever before, even in what often is a less-inviting environment at home. I believe that soul winning on an overseas mission field will keep a person excited about winning souls back home in their own country. First Baptist, Daytona Beach's, international mission advance has now become formalized with staff, budget, policies, and goals.

Our basic goal is to send out one team of volunteers to an overseas mission location each month. The teams are away for at least a week and up to a month. We desire to have a Report/Commissioning service each month where the team coming home is welcomed and gives its report. The team going out is prayed over and sent out. Currently, we have eight overseas mission trips a year. The teams involve themselves in crusades, revivals, church building, evangelism clinics, FAITH clinics, sport clinics, medical work, surveys, VBS, and a multiplicity of other efforts. Regardless of the nature of any of our mission endeavors, soul-winning evangelism has a priority as a result of FAITH training and its philosophy of ministry.

We have had other churches join with us to participate and to observe. Some have been stimulated to adopt a mission advance strategy in their own churches. One such church now has a goal of building 100 soul winning churches along with several children's homes on international fields over the next 10 years. First Baptist, Daytona Beach, through our "Beyond the Continent" strategy has over the last three years become a part of an effort to build 100 churches on the mission field and expects to see the 100th church built on July 31, 1998. Most everyone who goes on our overseas mission trips has participated in FAITH prior to going. FAITH not only gets those volunteer missionaries prepared to go around the world with the gospel, it provides a place for them to continue their ministry upon returning home.

It is probable that multiplied thousands of believers who begin their journey on a basic FAITH Team as a FAITH Learner will find themselves going to mission locations in far-away lands. They usually will be speaking through translators, and they will lead and train Christians and churches to do FAITH in that country. I know that will happen because our church has been doing it for years in Africa, Russia, Brazil, Ecuador, Honduras, Caribbean, and India. The people in your church deserve that opportunity. All of what I have described will not happen the first year. Some results within each of the four areas of expected results will happen in the first year, however.

Usually, numerical church growth occurs first along with spiritual growth beginning to surface, followed by developing local ministry burden. Then, an expanded mission advance will begin to stir. FAITH has a tremendous enriching and enhancing ability.

It may be hard for you to believe that this is possible. FAITH will do it, however, and you'll enjoy inevitable results. We at First Baptist took a 23-year journey to develop and arrive at what is now called the FAITH Sunday School evangelism ministry. It has been an exciting and God-led trip. You'll appreciate the experience and reap the rewards.

I know that will happen because our church has been doing it for years in Africa, Russia, Brazil, Ecuador, Honduras, Caribbean, and India.

DAYTONA—A PROVEN EXPERIENCE

FAITH is not an idea hatched out in a brainstorming session. It germinated in the rocky soil of a tough church field. FAITH is the product of the work of a congregation and staff committed to the Great Commission as their command and with a sincere determination to try to win their world in their lifetime. It evolved out of 23 years of one pastor at one church in an unusual situation, but it is effective for any pastor at any church of any size.

SITUATION

Daytona Beach is a city of about 64,000 people. There is another 100,000 who live in surrounding communities. The area is almost totally dependent upon tourism and has two predominate faces—one of a laid back family vacation spot and the other as a party town. There are times when the area almost seems to shut down because of the lack of visitors.

Our church is in the geographic center of the old downtown area. We have all the attendant problems: we must hire security patrolmen, need more parking, own fewer than five acres, land is extremely expensive around us. Everyone who attends our church must drive a considerable distance and drive past one or more other churches to get to us downtown.

There are two other major obstacles to our growth potential. One, our church field consists of only one-half of a circle because our church is located near the Atlantic Ocean's edge. To add to that trouble, our city has developed north and south of the church, further eliminating another pie wedge from our church field circle. Until presently, with perhaps one exception, no sizable residential development has been built within seven miles of our church in over 20 years. Ours is not an ideal spot from which to grow a strong church.

The second additional major obstacle to church growth here is that of the spiritual climate. Testimonies from the past and my 23 years of experience confirm the existence of a serious spiritual lack throughout the area.

Good news! God knows where we are, and we know what He desires for His church to do regardless of the less-than-favorable circumstances and situations. If First Baptist, Daytona Beach, can not only survive but thrive, so can your church. FAITH is the centerpiece for that success. God Almighty is waiting for you to take a step to let Him get loose where you are.

BEFORE

The process to FAITH has taken a lengthy journey, but when you adapt FAITH to your Sunday School and church, you will reap the benefits of our 23 years of trial, error, and refinement. From our situation, we set out to do the Great Commission and win our world as well as grow in Christ individually.

My first week as the church's 31-year-old pastor, I preached, prayed, promoted, and pleaded for the membership to come out on Thursday to go visiting for Jesus and the church. The result was less than exciting. The people did not respond to my intentions to go to peoples' homes and encourage them personally to come to church and Sunday School. On the first day of visitation 18 people came. The next week only three came.

The result was less than exciting.

We began to search for an effective way to enlist, train, and motivate our people so they might grow in Christlikeness and be faithful to the Great Commission as a church and as individuals. During those first months and years, our visitation force gradually grew, and our Sunday School began to advance. Despite the successes, there always was the haunting thought in my heart that something was missing.

NEXT

From those earliest stages we began to do better in preparing and organizing our visitation assignments but had little coordination of visitation with Sunday School. During that time, we did all sorts of training programs to try to equip and encourage our people to learn how to visit and then to come and go visit. We used weekend training courses, one-night courses, two- and three-night courses, one-week courses, the Church Training hour courses, pulpit preaching, Saturday courses, Sunday afternoon courses, and a host of others. We offered visitation times in the morning and at night. We included the *Roman Road,* the *Four Spiritual Laws,* the *Law of the Harvest,* the WIN School, and several of our own developments. We had emphases and encouragements ranging from banners to suppers. I often preached prolonged series on visitation and soul winning. Not a single one of those things was harmful, and all of them helped us. Yet, we would go up and then go down over and over.

I called this type of outreach "Y'all Come" visitation.

Eventually, the Lord blessed us. We sometimes had a high of over 100 people out to visitation per week. That was a respectable number and a good percentage of our Sunday School. I called this type of outreach "Y'all Come" visitation. People came to visitation when they could, which was not the level of commitment it would take to do what we needed to do in our situation.

Now, here is an important point. Even if we had been able to have an adequate, sustained number to go visiting, we still would have shortchanged our people because of the lack of depth of materials, accountability, hands-on training, and discipleship that the fully developed FAITH ministry provides. But, we had not arrived at FAITH in those days. We were being led that way, however.

Our Sunday School continued to grow but was moving into a period of plateauing and a likely stagnation. We were working hard, deeply concerned, and by all accounts doing the right things. What would happen? What would we do? Like before, deep inside of me I knew something was missing. Would it ever come together the way I was convinced it should and could?

FINALLY

Eight years had passed, and then I came to sense what I thought was a difference in evangelism training and visitation that would move us closer to where we should be in training, discipleship, and soul winning. What we were doing was not strong in some parts, especially Sunday School, public confession, and baptism, but that would be remedied. Doug Williams and his wife, Rachel, joined our staff. Doug and I had been friends for a long time, and I knew he had dedicated himself to the ministry of evangelism for the local Baptist church. That circumstance brought some promising ingredients together. One of the key moves for us was to make our evangelism training ministry the one and only evangelism outreach approach for our church. My feelings were that we could never get to our best results if we were fragmented in our approaches. We were considerate and careful in making this transition over a year-long process.

The staff took the leadership right from the start and gave our best efforts to lead the church to put in the needed commitment and work. It was not long until we all could see the benefits in a number of ways. Our people valued the investment this approach demanded of their personal spiritual lives, and they appreciated our punctual schedules and the initial class materials and teaching techniques. They were becoming effective witnesses, and the people they met, knew, and loved were getting saved.

As pastor, I was grateful that all the involvement did not now

The people they met, knew, and loved were getting saved.

rest upon my preaching and enlistment abilities. Our new approach had a distinguishing way of enlistment coupled with the team accountability factor that made the difference.

We developed and continue to conduct two 16-week STEPS, fall and spring, which eliminated my frustration with the up-and-down cycles of "Y'all Come" visitation. We have realized that with absences and schedule conflicts, it is not possible for persons to get in enough training in a program lasting less than 16 weeks.

Sunday School was still only incidentally and accidentally connected to our evangelism ministry in the beginning. Our staff persons are "team players" with gracious spirits, but that does not mean we were not headed for the collision of Sunday School and evangelism. We still were aware that something was missing.

NOW

After years of perfecting our approach, there came the time we had been searching for—we combined Sunday School and evangelism.

After years of perfecting our approach, there came the time we had been searching for—we combined Sunday School and evangelism. What could have been more obvious and promising? We mated the largest organization of the church that is doing small-group Bible teaching with the visitation ministry that is doing evangelism. When that coupling of the two was done, the visitation teams were assigned visits to those members of a Sunday School class for the purpose of maintaining, nurturing, caring, and keeping those already won as well as prospect evangelism. The ministry began to benefit Sunday school classes immediately, which made everyone enthusiastic. At this junction, the visitation teams no longer were called evangelism teams but E/S teams because their training, mission, and assignments had to do with both evangelism and Sunday School. It was at that point we all recognized that we had finally found that something that had been missing!

Since that marriage of our Sunday School and evangelism over 12 years ago, we are happy to report that the couple has continued to fall more deeply in love with each other. Each has come to appreciate and admire the other more and more and cannot imagine life separated one from the other.

Is anyone wondering about that concerning your church? Yes, there really is a marriage made in heaven just waiting to happen at your own church. Don't you think someone should stand up and unite this lovely, dynamic, and God-called couple at your church?

The name changed from E/S to FAITH Sunday School evangelism training solely because the gospel presentation portion of the outline needed to be more closely connected to Sunday School and public confession of faith in Christ. FAITH Sunday School evangelism training is a process and procedure of which the gospel presentation is but one component. Of course, it is a key part and has an unusual ability to connect a person with the Sunday School. Regardless, if a person receives Christ or does not, FAITH will attach them to Sunday School. Also, we desired a winsome and effective way to bring those who did receive Christ to make a public profession at the church and then be baptized.

The public commitment encouragement comes as a part of *A Journey Toward Faith,* the booklet that is used immediately after a person prays to receive Christ. In that booklet, the person is led through three clear steps to a public commitment. This public commitment is tied to the last part of the prayer the person prayed moments before he or she received Christ.

All of this was set in motion from the beginning when the visiting FAITH team dealt with the prospect's Sunday School involvement and then gave their "Sunday School Testimony." The opening and closing portions of the outline were named PREPARATION and INVITATION respectively. Also, the gospel presentation portion, called PRESENTATION, was completely changed. It is tied to Sunday School, public confession, and baptism. The actual PRESENTATION portion of the outline comes through an acronym based upon the word FAITH and centered upon a powerful visual.

As I have reviewed the record, it is clear to me that if our church had not combined Sunday School with evangelism, we were destined for a downward plunge in Sunday School attendance and baptisms. Interestingly, we have compared the progress of our church for 20 years to that of what could be an identical church. That church dropped its evangelism training program at about the same time we combined Sunday School and evangelism to avoid our downward plunge. That church went into a nose dive in almost every way, especially in Sunday School attendance and baptisms. My observation is that what we've come to call FAITH Sunday School evangelism ministry is what prevented us from the same fate and has us moving toward the 2,000 average in Sunday School. FAITH has done all that and more for us and can do the same for any church.

WHAT ABOUT OTHER VISITATION PROGRAMS?

Surely someone will ask, "Can such benefits come by using a

If our church had not combined Sunday School with evangelism, we were destined for a downward plunge in Sunday School attendance and baptisms.

similar evangelism ministry approach other than the FAITH model?"

The truth is that any approach that consistently engages Christians in witnessing to lost people will produce results. FAITH, however, is far and away the most productive approach I have ever seen. It is a comprehensive ministry to win our world in our lifetime through the local church's Sunday School. Evangelism materials for Baptist needs have been written and published based on our model. All FAITH training clinics and materials will use those materials. Consequently, it will be possible to create a true FAITH ministry within your Sunday School and church by using only the materials that are incorporated into this particular approach.

STEVE COLEMAN

YOUNG ADULT I
SUNDAY SCHOOL
CLASS

Helping Needs

Two years ago, as a result of the FAITH ministry, I was led to the Lord. At that time, I had a good understanding of what salvation is, but as time went by, I had problems explaining it to a person with the use of scriptural references. I was once asked by a coworker who was of a denomination that doesn't believe in personal salvation where the Bible says anything about being saved. I didn't have an answer for him.

Now that I've been through this program, I have the ability to present the gospel with confidence and to communicate its true meaning.

I've also been inspired by the commitment of the instructors and trainers as I came to know them during the 16 weeks. One of the things that particularly stood out was the tireless efforts of Mary Anne Rodgers. She led our team with a standard of professionalism. Each week as we witnessed, I noticed that she was always helping somebody. She would sometimes have in her car groceries for another family or a car seat for a child she was taking care of.

Those things didn't go unnoticed. I am glad I had the opportunity to witness, learn, and work with such devoted people.

OUR FUTURE AND ASSIMILATION

When FAITH opens the heart and eyes of the souls who make up your fellowship and Jesus gets loose within them, the future is going to become breathtaking for you and the entire church! It most certainly has been for First Baptist, Daytona Beach! We should have dried up like many others in our downtown neighborhood. Instead, we are alive, well, thriving, and on fire for His future through us, our Sunday School, and our church. We have a dream, a vision, a plan, and a concrete belief that we can win our world in our lifetime! Of course, FAITH is not the only thing contributing to our spirit, but it is the stack pole upon which all else leans. It has set the pace and tone and established the atmosphere that permeates the life of all else.

The future is going to become breathtaking for you and the entire church!

Predicated upon what I've shared in this section about the First Baptist, Daytona Beach, experience, let me give a simple overview of our church's thrilling future, which can be a foreshadowing of any church's future.

Here is what we have concluded and committed to for our future:

• To define, focus, strategize, commit, and act in the ministry areas where through the years God has been directing and shaping our fellowship. That is, to ACKNOWLEDGE where God has already been working and blessing through our church's ministry life and to ACT in ways that will result in us winning our world in our lifetime. Simply said, "We will organize and commit to do better what we have been led of God to do in recent years."

• To accomplish our goal, our church's ministry work has been separated into four divisions. We found those directions to be compatible with God's plan in Acts 1:8: "Ye shall receive power, after that the Holy Ghost is come upon you: and ye shall be witnesses unto me both in Jerusalem, and in all Judaea, and in Samaria, and unto the uttermost part of the earth."

First Baptist Church, Daytona Beach's Ministry:

1. At the church (Jerusalem)
2. In the city (Judaea)
3. Across this country (Samaria)
4. Beyond the continent (uttermost parts of the earth)

Each of the ministry divisions will be energized and driven by what we call EVERY MEMBER MINISTRY WITH PRIORITY.

1. First Baptist's ministry AT THE CHURCH (JERUSALEM) means that we will continue to do at the church the same kinds of effective ministries that God has been blessing. We clearly defined and listed those. Our ministry at the church must stay strong.

2. First Baptist's ministry IN THE CITY (JUDAEA) will be those efforts to win and minister to people who probably would never enter the door of our church. Those things we will do to reach more of those 140,000 unchurched and unsaved we are driving past each week on the way to the church. A list of ministries has been defined for "in the city." These ministries always will have additions, deletions, and adjustments as we continue to discover how best to win our world in our lifetime IN THE CITY.

3. First Baptist's ministry ACROSS THIS COUNTRY (SAMARIA) refers to our church's considerable sacrifice and contributions made in partnership with The Sunday School Board to win America in our lifetime through the FAITH ministry approach.

4. First Baptist's ministry BEYOND THE CONTINENT (UTTERMOST PARTS OF THE EARTH) focuses on our mission work overseas. We had been doing a good job at this already, but our future will have this international effort organized, staffed, budgeted, and increased. We will accelerate what we had been doing overseas until we have a mission team going from our church and one returning from the field each month. Our overseas mission goal is also to win our world in our lifetime.

> Effective evangelistic churches have both their mission and vision of ministry emphasize evangelism. Everything they do has an evangelistic flavor to it. Yet, these churches are not driven by numbers. They see success as being faithful to share the gospel, not in the number of decisions recorded. (George Barna, *Florida Baptist Witness*, March 7, 1996).

EVERY MEMBER MINISTRY WITH PRIORITY is a vital aspect of our approach to our future. When a person becomes a member of the church, he or she is assigned, through an interview process, to two small groups: (1) a Sunday School class and (2) a ministry team. Immediately upon joining, the person then is connected to two friends, the FAITH Facilitator and the FAITH Team Leader, who will talk and meet with them. Also, the new member now has an ownership and contribution through a meaningful ministry that assists the church to reach its overall goal. Barna's research has confirmed earlier facts that a majority of people who make decisions to become Christians have dropped out of church participation within six to eight weeks. One of the purposes of the two small groups is to keep that from happening.

A new member joins our church, selects a ministry team, does that particular ministry, enables Division 1, 2, 3, and 4 to achieve its goal, and ultimately has a personal part in the church accomplishing its overall goal. The person also is in a Sunday School class at the same time. Those members participating in the two small groups are recognized as active members.

The priority of the every member ministry effort is found in 1 Corinthians 9:19-23. These ministry teams are to be all things to all people, having made themselves servant types for the ultimate end, that they "might by all means save some."

A story is told about years ago when John Henry Giles wanted to preach a sermon on "The Wind Blows Where It Will." He went down to the docks of his city and asked an old sailor friend, a seasoned salt with a weather-beaten face, to tell him about the wind. He wanted to discover where the wind came from, how the wind works, and how to control the wind. His old seaman friend mused, "Oh, Preacher, I don't know the answer to those questions. I don't know where the wind comes from. I don't know how the wind works. And I sure don't know how to control the wind."

"You mean to tell me," responded the preacher, "that you have sailed the seven seas, you have spent your life living by the winds, and you don't know those things?"

"No, Preacher," answered the old sailor, "I don't know how the wind works, but I do know one thing. I know how to hoist my sail to catch the wind. And when I do, it takes me wherever I need to go."

Let us hoist the sail called FAITH and catch the wind of the Holy Spirit and go into the 21st century with a life and a church on fire to win our world in our lifetime!

RESTORING A BIRTHRIGHT

A hurried glance through writings of early Sunday School Board leaders yields evidence that they understood that part of their birthright was to soul-winning evangelism.

> "The Sunday School has the message which is the Power of God unto salvation for everyone who believes. The officers and teachers in Sunday School constitute the church's greatest bank of soul winners and trainers of soul winners. More and more churches are realizing the possibilities for evangelism which lie in a properly functioning Sunday School." (J. N. Barnette, 1945)
>
> "The Sunday School is formed and operated for the purpose of winning the lost." (J. N. Barnette, 1945)
>
> "The whole Sunday School is designed to contribute directly and continuously to evangelism." (J. N. Barnette, 1945)

> "The Sunday School leads all church members to witness daily, to worship daily, and to minister daily." (A. V. Washburn, 1964)
>
> "The business of a Sunday school is to reach and to teach the people." (J. N. Barnette, 1955)
>
> "No apology is necessary for a frequent repetition of reaching, teaching, and winning people. These are the heart and soul of Sunday School work." (J. N. Barnette, 1937)

The early portion of the 20th century was replete with great books on how to build a thriving Sunday School. Scholars and practitioners placed before churches of their generation vital information about the values of building a strong and vigorous Bible study organization. One of the classic resources was *Building a Successful Sunday School*[3] by P. E. Burroughs.

Burroughs set forth on page 178 two basic tenets regarding how one measures a successful Sunday School. "The Sunday School which lays claim to success must do two things: (1) It must reach its constituency and (2) It must teach its constituency. It can hardly be said that one of these things is more important than the other, since they are interdependent. We cannot teach people unless we reach them; when we reach people we will almost certainly teach them."

As one reads relevant books from another period, the references listed accent the honor given to personal evangelism in the Bible study organization. Here are just a few:

- *With Christ After the Lost,* by Lee Rutland Scarborough
- *Winning to Christ—A Study in Evangelism,* by Prince Emanual Burroughs
- *Pastoral and Personal Evangelism,* by Charles L. Goodell
- *Passion for Souls,* by John Henry Jowett

Our generation has been negligent in placing importance on the task of soul winning through the Sunday School. Is it any wonder that thousands of our churches go through a calendar year without having one person among them come to know Christ as Savior?

Bible studies and Sunday School organizations that are considered successful in the 21st century will be no different from the earlier churches. They must reach people if they are to be considered on the cutting edge of ministry.

"The soul-winning spirit, the evangelistic effort, must constitute the salt which is to save and keep sweet our growing Sunday Schools." P. E. Burroughs

The point is that today's leaders of The Sunday School Board have concluded that their historical and foundational birthright of "soul winning" must be restored to its rightful place within the Sunday School with maximum emphasis alongside that of the Sunday School's teaching ministry. The FAITH ministry is the boldest declaration of that fact. FAITH will equip the Sunday School to effect the biblical model of New Testament ministry through the cycle of Follow—Learn—Teach.

"We believe that every Sunday School and church should implement, as quickly as possible, the FAITH ministry. We have been praying, planning, and promoting this all-out effort to equip every Sunday School to win their world in their lifetime through FAITH. Already the next years of our work are projected and based upon this innovative, effective, and proven approach. We earnestly believe FAITH is the best way to revolutionize our Sunday Schools, not just to survive but thrive to the glory of God in the 21st century!" Dr. James Draper, Dr. Gene Mims, Dr. Bill Taylor

RETURN TO THE BIBLICAL MODEL

There appears to be two models of discipleship life before us.

 The **BIBLICAL MODEL** is what we call the one that reflects the New Testament mandate for ministry described in God's Word. This model is demonstrated by Jesus, His apostles, and His disciples in the first-century church. This model follows a cycle. First, Jesus would call the person to FOLLOW. Then, the followers would LEARN as they went with Jesus. They then would TEACH and train others in what they had learned while they followed Christ. The cycle rotated around FOLLOW—LEARN—TEACH. It was an unending cycle with no indication that a believer was to only FOLLOW but not learn and then teach. Nor only to FOLLOW and LEARN but not also teach and train. Neither is there a suggestion that a disciple was to FOLLOW—LEARN—TEACH and at some point say, "I've done that" and stop learning or stop teaching.

No, none of those options were to be exercised. The FOLLOW—LEARN—TEACH cycle was to be ongoing for the length of the follower's life. This was not a "project" approach but an ongoing ministry and life. The followers of Christ were on their non-ending equipping journey to become Great Commission Christians. The following verses substantiate that:

Mark 1:17: "Jesus said unto them, Come ye after me, and I will make you to become fishers of men."

Second Timothy 2:2: "The things that thou hast heard of me among many witnesses, the same commit thou to faithful men, who shall be able to teach others also."

Mark 16:15: "He said unto them, Go ye into all the world, and preach the gospel to every creature."

Matthew 28:18-20: "Jesus came and spake unto them, saying, All power is given unto me in heaven and in earth. Go ye therefore, and teach all nations, baptizing them in the name of the Father, and of the Son, and of the Holy Ghost: Teaching them to observe all things whatsoever I have commanded you: and lo, I am with you alway, even unto the end of the world."

Luke 24:47-48: "Repentance and remission of sins should be preached in his name among all nations, beginning at Jerusalem. And ye are witnesses of these things."

John 20:21: "Then said Jesus to them again, Peace be unto you: as my Father hath sent me, even so send I you."

Acts 1:8: "Ye shall receive power, after that the Holy Ghost is come upon you: and ye shall be witnesses unto me both in Jerusalem, and in all Judaea, and in Samaria, and unto the uttermost part of the earth."

The subject matter for this cycle of FOLLOW—LEARN—TEACH is unmistakably SOUL WINNING EVANGELISM. Other areas of a disciple's life will go through this same cycle. Unless soul winning evangelism is actively recurring in a believer who continues to FOLLOW—LEARN—TEACH, all other areas are but unfinished business. Mark 16:15 says, "He said unto them. Go ye unto all the world, and preach the gospel to every creature." This verse and others give us God's Great Commission that is to be accomplished by His followers. They can only accomplish this by making the cycle of FOLLOW—LEARN—TEACH a lifetime commitment with priority upon soul winning.

Another model has emerged that critically departs from and abandons the BIBLICAL MODEL. We title it the PRESENT DAY MODEL because it appears to be the dominating model at this time within Christendom. I'm sure there are churches that do not fit the PRESENT DAY MODEL. They are rare, however.

The **PRESENT DAY MODEL** encourages church attendees to accept Christ as their Savior. Some will go so far as to urge them to FOLLOW Jesus, but that following will have little emphasis upon the LEARN and TEACH part of the disciple's life. If the LEARN aspect is promoted, it usually is done only by study groups, and the subject matter is overwhelmingly focused inwardly upon those in the study group. There most often is only a passing interest in the lost of the world. There is no on-the-job training. Further, those involved in the PRESENT DAY MODEL feel little responsibility or obligation to teach and train others as did the first-century disciples as they were admonished to do in 2 Timothy 2:2. This PRESENT DAY MODEL has forfeited the two most distinguishing characteristics of the early church and its followers. They learned soul winning, and then they trained other soul winners. The majority of present-day churches, including Southern Baptists and other evangelical churches, do not provide any ongoing way for their members to learn how to be effective soul winners. Neither is there any way for them to train others to be soul winners.

There is no scriptural support or comfort apparent for this unfortunate model that has stagnated us in winning our world. Largely because of that, we Southern Baptists have come to the end of this 20th century with the past 16 years "flat lined" in the one thing Jesus told us to do—win souls.

Ask yourself two questions. First, "Which of the two models presented am I personally practicing now?" Second, "Which of the two models is most obviously practiced on an ongoing basis in my church?

FAITH Sunday School evangelism ministry will give you the right method to put 1st century discipleship into your 21st century Sunday School and church.

WHY CHANGE WHAT WE'RE DOING NOW?

Because of church location, a specialty ministry, or other advantage, some churches grow even though they are not practicing the New Testament model. The question must be asked, "Are the members of the church growing into Great Commission Christians, according to the command of Jesus?

A man had been a committed and effectual soul winner and actively helped teach others as well. He moved and became a member of a fast-growing church in a booming suburb. Afterwards, he

Who Knows Where?

My enrollment in the Sunday School evangelism training has enabled me to strengthen my spiritual growth and enhance my knowledge of Scripture. That involvement has made me keenly aware of how many lost people I come in contact with on a daily basis.

I always thought that when I presented the gospel for the first time, it would be on Tuesday night during our visitation time. But after 11 weeks of training, I presented the gospel to my terminally ill mother-in-law in my home on Saturday morning. Three days later I visited a member of my staff who had just been told that he had only three months to live. I was able to present the gospel to him and to his wife as well.

I am so thankful that I heard God's call to enroll in the Sunday School evangelism training. I can now witness effectively when before, all I could do was feel the pain of not knowing what to do. Because of my training experience, I am prepared to share the best news I can ever share with anyone, the wonderful news of eternal life!

STEVE JOHNSTON

MEDIAN ADULT 3
SUNDAY SCHOOL
CLASS

PUBLIC ELEMENTARY
SCHOOL PRINCIPAL

told me he no longer really needed to witness or teach others because the church was growing so fast they did not need such an effort. He then said that the pastor had told the church that he, the staff, and a committee would talk to those presenting themselves for salvation. The man seemed happy and interpreted such a state of affairs as a spiritual step up from the days when members felt the conviction to go soul winning and churches trained others to do likewise.

My thought was that the church was growing too fast in the wrong direction. A growing Sunday School class or church does not release us from our individual mandate to witness and train others as an ongoing lifestyle.

What if a church had all the money it required for several months. Seeing that "growth condition," is the individual to jump to the ridiculous conclusion that tithing and offerings are no longer a scriptural truth that should apply to them personally? You and I cannot escape the fact that the Son of God was a personal soul winner, training others to be personal soul winners. He commanded us to do exactly the same, all around the world, beginning in our own community. Anyone growing away from that direction is growing in the wrong direction, no matter how much they grow. Such an approach is a "dumbing down" spiritually of disciples and "numbing down" of world evangelism!

TODAY'S SATANIC STRATEGY

Social revolutions are like sudden and violent disturbances in the weather. A sociologist senses their approach years in advance of the time when the full fury breaks. Prophets issue their warnings; wise students of history point out trends that are ominous. Isaiahs, Jeremiahs, and Hoseas warn the thoughtless populace about the disasters they are bringing upon themselves by their heedless disregard of the laws of God. Long before the evolution of human society was analyzed and the definite laws controlling it were discovered, God's prophets were inspired to know the relation between certain social trends and cataclysmic upheavals within the social body or an overwhelming oppression from without. Thus, they were compelled to seek and save people from ruinous downfall.

At this time and under present conditions, it is easy for many of us to see the shadows that are gathering over the Christian church. Today's evil strategy against the church is real. Some may debate the "Why," but the largest concern is the "How." How can it be observed?

My deep conviction is that this strategy is being perpetrated upon us in three phases.

Phase 1

MATERIALISM is what I would call Phase 1 of Satan's devices. This aspect centers on fun and is to soften up Christian leaders and laypeople. There was a time when the heroes of the faith were dedicated followers giving their all for Jesus. They were the models. More and more, the model is marked by what you get instead of what you give.

Today's Christians usually are attracted to churches that promote what their members will get if they attend. The church's approach tends to be "promise more and demand less."

Jesus made it undeniably clear that the world's way to success is not His way. He illustrated how those who operate by the world's standard of success get to the top by lording over many underlings. Then, in comparison, Jesus declared those inescapable words, "But it shall not be so among you" (Matt. 20:26).

Jesus said that we are to be servants (*diakonos*) if we are to be great and bondslaves (*doulos*) if we will be the greatest, according to Matthew 20:26-27).

Too much of the Christian leadership in the western world has been lured into and locked into the prison house of prosperity. Emphasis on prosperity and success not only has distracted us from the servant life, which Christ exemplified and to which He exhorts us, it has moved us away from soul winning to self-success, self-health, self-worth, and self-prosperity.

The life of Christ is not a call to a cushion but to a cross, not to a gold-plated boulevard named "Easy Street" or "Feather Bed" but to a dusty Galilean way distinguished by self-denial, sacrifice, suffering, and servanthood. Let us not trade our spiritual birthright as a servant for a mess of materialistic pottage called earthly success.

The strategy of Satan is to use materialism to "soften up" the church, the leaders, and the laypeople in preparation for Phase 2.

Phase 2

LEGAL issues are the next stage of satanic strategy for attacking today's church. First, we have been blanketed with an unparalleled wave of prosperity of materialism, and now Christians and individual churches are feeling the hot breath of intimidation by courts and lawyers.

What could not be done by fun and materialism may well be brought about by fear and intimidation. The forecast is that litigation is to increase. Churches are uniquely vulnerable in several ways and are perceived to have money and will do almost anything to avoid public embarrassment.

Litigation is just now coming into its own as the choice method to sanitize and sterilize schools, work place, and society of saints. You will be fascinated to observe that legal intimidation almost always occurs at the point of outreach and evangelism. You will hear members and leaders inside the church respond to a legal threatening situation by indicating it may be best not to try something or to do that anymore, referring to some outreach and evangelism possibility or effort. So, the fear of legal intimidation then has voices inside as well as outside the church that are in effect saying, "It would be safer and best to stay inside these church walls and mind our own business." Such acts are in direct opposition to the Great Commission, Jesus, and the Bible. Those efforts are to "scare off" the mighty army of God, to tear down strongholds that save our homes, children, marriages, and the lost of our world. We cannot give in to such!

Phase 3

"DEMONISM" is the third phase and perhaps the last-ditch, all-out, final assault upon us before the Second Coming of Christ. These three evil strategies are interlocking and overlapping. My opinion is that we are in the latter part of Phase 1's materialism and just entering Phase 2's legal assault upon the Christian's life, family, church, community, and Great Commission.

"Demonism" will not focus upon fun or fear but upon raw demonic *force*. It will be third in the progression from "soften up" to "scare off" to "shut us down." While America has indulged itself in an age of ungodliness, and while the body of Christ in America has relaxed and withdrawn itself, the forces of hell have been developing and building landing sites and assembly grounds for their demonic hoards of hell!

Not until recent years was there any widespread notice in this country of occult and satanic churches and other such cult groups that have demonic forces and spirits, at the heart of their worship and activities. That now has changed and will undoubtedly continue to increase.

We must understand the shadows that are gathering and be about our Father's business while it is still day, for the night will come when no one can work (John 9:4). Our church and this nation does not have any problem that hot-hearted, Spirit-filled soul winning will not cure. FAITH is the tool to put into the hearts, heads, and hands of Christians to do the work of ministry in a way that defies hell and defeats Satan. He that is within us is greater than He that is in the world (1 John 4:4), and FAITH is a way you can prove that through your own victorious life. Not only Satan's three-fold strategy but five frank facts that we must face should cause us to want to be fully equipped to help our family and those around us.

The body of Christ in America has relaxed and withdrawn itself.

Evangelism Through the Sunday School: A Journey of FAITH

Feelings and Emotions

Sunday School evangelism training gave me the courage to stand taller and prouder for a faith that so many of us fail in. I am not bold enough yet, but the growth in my spirituality has provided me the boldness I needed to take the baby steps toward my personal "Great Commission." I pray that through further training, I and many more will be making the giant steps that the Lord expects from us to carry out His love through the sharing of it and the gospel.

Social, spiritual, comical, serious, loving, heart-wrenching, soul-searching, eye-opening, strengthening—all those and more describe some of the feelings and emotions that have been brought to the surface of my soul through the training ministry experience, and I can't thank God enough for that.

SHARON BOYER

MEDIAN ADULT 6
SUNDAY SCHOOL
CLASS

BUSINESS OWNER,
DENTAL OFFICE

FIVE FRANK FACTS

"I will say to the reapers, Gather ye together first the tares, and bind them in bundles to burn them: but gather the wheat into my barn" (Matt. 13:30).

I want to offer you Five Frank Facts that should urge you to witness and win your own family, friends, and your world. I am indebted to the late Oswald T. Smith who first got me to thinking about such facts. These facts will encourage you to get involved in the FAITH ministry.

FRANK FACT 1: NOT ALL PEOPLE WILL BE SAVED

The Universalists are wrong! They believe that everyone is going to heaven eventually no matter what they do or how they live. This belief is widespread, and many people believe and act that way. It is not true; God's Word is clear on that point.

Jesus frankly declared in the parable of the tares (weeds) that all will not enter the kingdom and heaven (Matt. 13:24-30). All people will not be saved. That is not God and Christ's choice or desire, but it is a frank fact.

That is not God and Christ's choice or desire, but it is a frank fact.

Persons will profess Christ in their homes but won't come forward at church. Perhaps they do come forward and are baptized. They may get into Sunday School classes and work in the church. Then, they fall away and perhaps go back to their old lifestyles. What do you say about that? I can tell you what the devil will say. He'll slip up to the ear of your heart and say, "You are wasting your time. Why, you don't know weeds from seeds!" When you get to thinking that way, remember where it came from. God didn't give you that thought. That idea came right out of the pit of hell to stop you from witnessing.

That's one of the strengths of FAITH. You are exposed to a steady flow of spiritual victories that are happening to both those in the ministry and those to whom we minister. This approach keeps in plain view the many exciting blessings that overshadow any discouragement.

A few years back a pastor stopped me at a Convention meeting and asked if I knew a certain man. My reply was No, I did not. He proceeded to describe the man and told me that the man and I had served together in a Green Beret paratrooper military unit and that I had been the officer over the enlisted man. I still could not remember the man. Finally, the preacher went ahead with his story. He said that the young man had hopped into the back seat of my vehicle as another man and I pulled away to go board an airplane for a parachute jump. The pastor further told me that the young man said that I had clearly presented the gospel to the rider in the front seat but that the man did not pray to accept Christ when I offered him the opportunity.

By this time I was wondering, "Why is this pastor telling me this?" Then, he made his point. The preacher said, "That young man who was in the back seat that day is a member of my church. He told me to tell you that although the man in the front seat did not pray with you to be saved, he did while in the back seat!" The pastor went on to thrill my soul by saying, "Not only had this 'unknown soldier' been saved, he was called to preach and went to a seminary!"

What if that day I had said, "Lord, if someone doesn't truly accept Christ today, I'm going to stop trying to witness." I would have made a foolish and tragic mistake! God is at work, so just be faithful, and one day you'll be astounded at what He has done through your witnessing.

All will not be saved, but we must sow all the seed we can.

FRANK FACT 2: THE MAJORITY WILL BE LOST

"Enter ye in at the strait gate: for wide is the gate, and broad is the way, that leadeth to destruction, and many there be which go in thereat" (Matt. 7:13).

I became concerned when I first read that Scripture verse. I got my Greek New Testament. I got a lexicon and my Bible word studies, and I looked up that word "many." I discovered the Greek meaning. It means "many"! It means exactly what it says. It means many—an abundance—a large amount—the vast majority. Jesus said that the majority of the people in this life are going to be lost without Christ. The Bible is true. It means exactly what it says. Jesus said that many—most—the majority are going to be lost and not be saved.

That brings me to the question I hear: "How can God stand by and let the majority of people plunge into hellfire for eternity? How can God allow that to happen?" Well, remember that everybody makes his or her own choice. You and I are choosing today. If you are not a Christian, you are choosing to follow that way. You could choose to be saved. You could choose to follow the Lord. So, when we choose to go to heaven, we've chosen to agree with God and Jesus and go to heaven. If you want to go to hell, choose the other way.

If you want to go to hell, all you've got to do is nothing. Just sit there where you are—keep on depending on being good to your neighbor—depend on Grandma and Grandpa—depend on your tithe, baptism, and church—depend on being a good boy or girl—depend on paying your taxes—depend on such as that and do nothing in regard to Jesus. Guess where you'll end up. Not in heaven.

Do you know why most people are going to be eternally lost? Because there are not more of us saved people who care about them. When statistics reveal that about 50 percent of people are won because of their family and friends, that should stimulate us to want to share the gospel. It should make us want to learn how to reach our friends and our family with the gospel of Jesus Christ. We should do that because it's a frank fact that the majority of people will be lost. That will be changed when believers begin to win the majority of their family and friends.

FRANK FACT 3: MANY WILL PERISH WHO EXPECT TO BE SAVED

"Not every one that saith unto me, Lord, Lord, shall enter into the kingdom of heaven; but he that doeth the will of my Father which is in heaven" (Matt. 7:21).

The first part of this verse is one of the key verses in the FAITH gospel presentation. It stresses the fact that forgiveness of sin is not automatic and no one should assume it is. A legitimate question is asked, "Where are all those people on church membership rolls who never attend church?" There are several answers to that, but one must be that many of them are not truly saved Christian people. That truth would also encompass some on the church roll who do attend. The FAITH ministry strives to ensure that those who come to unite with your congregation and those in the church are indeed saved.

Jesus said that many will perish who are expecting to be saved. That's the saddest part of the story. There are many people who think they are going to be saved, but they are going to perish because they don't know Jesus Christ as their Savior and Lord.

The only remedy for that pitiful condition is not our intelligence and not our logic. The only key is the power of the Holy Spirit working through an individual who knows how to share the Lord Jesus Christ. That's what FAITH enables you to do. It doesn't call you to participate in a program of the church. It doesn't call you to be a friend to the preacher. It calls you to do what you can where God has planted you. The call is to learn and train in order for you not to fail to do your part to lead people to Christ. It is your opportunity to keep the "many" out of hell and show them how to get to heaven.

FRANK FACT 4: THERE IS NO SALVATION AFTER DEATH

"Beside all this, between us and you there is a great gulf fixed: so that they which would pass from hence to you cannot; neither can they pass to us, that would come from thence" (Luke 16:26).

Evangelism Through the Sunday School: A Journey of FAITH

That verse of Scripture is a powerful, shocking, startling reality. Jesus said that one person goes to heaven and one person goes to hell. In hell, one burns in torment and will plead for somebody to give relief.

Isn't it interesting that as soon as the man in the Scripture passage got to hell, his attitude completely changed. His heart broke. He looked toward God. He was humble. He called out and pleaded for help. He wanted to be a soul winner so that his family members would not end up in that horrible place called hell. Then, the bad news came; there is no help for anyone after they are in hell. There is a "great gulf fixed." That gulf is fixed and cannot be changed. Once you are on the other side of that fixed gulf, you cannot cross back over it.

Some sincere people will have others believe that there is some hope after death, a way for the lost to better themselves. That cannot be found in the Bible, and nowhere in Scripture will you find Jesus promoting that error. THERE IS NO SALVATION AFTER DEATH. No, there is not one slim glimmer or glimpse of hope for any lost person after this life. Those who have not been saved while upon this earth will not ever be saved. Thus, you and I must be witnessing and winning our world.

FRANK FACT 5: THIS MAY BE YOUR LAST OPPORTUNITY

"Boast not thyself of to morrow; for thou knowest not what a day may bring forth" (Prov. 27:1).

We are not to be bragging about what we'll do tomorrow because we don't know if we'll get through this day alive. Before this year is over many people will leave your acquaintance and go out into eternity without Christ. Time is a precious thing, but it runs out!

Beloved, listen, the Bible says that we'd better not brag about what time we've got left. We must take seriously this day because time runs out and opportunity gets away.

Seems to me that there are at least four reasons that time runs out and we miss our opportunity.

(1) If I die and have not used my opportunity, then time is lost.

(2) If the people who need to hear the gospel die, that ends my opportunity to reach them.

(3) Jesus could come back anytime, and that means my opportunity would be lost.

(4) The Spirit of God could cease to deal with the lost person, and that means I waited too long and my opportunity is lost.

Regardless of the reasons, we know how fragile life is and how quickly it goes. I was called to the death bed of a lady. Her daughter said, "I wish I had been here sooner to say one last word to her." Time had run out; the daughter's last word had been said. That day comes to all of us. We must not miss our opportunity to win our world.

Jimmie came only one time to Sunday School and church. Then, the young boy was struck by a car and killed in front of his home. I stood by his father's side at the funeral home. A thin veil had been draped over Jimmie's face because of his massive injuries. The father's tears made a puddle on the veil as they filtered through it and softly laid upon Jimmie's cheek. My arm was over the father's shoulders as he prayed to receive Christ in that spot.

The following Sunday, I met with the teachers and workers who had Jimmie in their class the Sunday before. Although it was Jimmie's first Sunday, he had been old enough to understand his need for Christ. Fortunately, he had a teacher who was equipped to recognize that need. The teacher knew how to interpret the boy's concerns and led him to receive Christ. Then, he suddenly was killed.

My meeting with the teachers and workers was to thank them for not missing their opportunity. It was Jimmie's last opportunity, and it was also their last opportunity. They did not miss that last opportunity. We shouldn't either.

All of these FIVE FRANK FACTS should urge us to begin and continue a ministry like FAITH because of the results we can expect and the difference we can make for now and eternity.

---

[1]Gene Mims, *Kingdom Principles for Church Growth* (Nashville: Convention Press, 1994).

[2]Donald Atkinson and Charles L. Roesel, *Meeting Needs, Sharing Christ* (Nashville: LifeWay Press, 1995).

[3]Bill Taylor, "Leader Lines," *The Sunday School Leader* (April 1997): 6.

[4]P. E. Burroughs, *Building a Successful Sunday School* (New York: Fleming H. Revel, Company, 1921), 29.

In Any Language

I was born into a Japanese Buddhist family. After coming to the United States, I became a Mormon. In the early 80s, I and my husband, Bill (who had been a bishop in the Mormon church for 12 years), were both saved and joined First Baptist Church, Daytona Beach.

When the Sunday School evangelism training began, we enrolled. I had a more difficult time with the studies because I needed to translate the thoughts from Japanese into English.

As I began to grow in my newfound faith, I became burdened for my family back in Japan, especially my mother, who was approaching 90 years of age. I translated the gospel presentation I had learned into Japanese and mailed it to my mother. After reading my letter many times and talking to me on the phone, Mother trusted in Christ. A comforting thing for me is that my mother closed our last phone conversation in Japanese with, "I'll see you in heaven, Terry."

I have continued in the training for 14 years and have served as a Team Leader here and in clinics in Russia and South Africa.

TERUKO
(TERRY) COATES

ADULT OUTREACH
LEADER AND
2ND GRADE
SUNDAY SCHOOL
TEACHER

BEAUTICIAN,
BUSINESS OWNER

PART 3

How Does FAITH Work?

"Effective evangelistic churches
PROVIDE GOOD EVANGELISM TRAINING
THROUGHOUT THE YEAR AND TEACH COURSES
AT DIFFERENT LEVELS."
—George Barna, *Florida Baptist Witness*, March 7, 1996

BILL GUNN

SENIOR ADULT 6
SUNDAY SCHOOL
DIRECTOR

Shirking Responsibility

Having been in church visitation programs many years, I still was never successful in leading someone to a profession of faith. That was the result of not being properly trained. Many times over the years I invited people to church, thinking the altar call would be sufficient to bring about their conversion. After several weeks of Sunday School evangelism training, the realization hit me that I had been shirking my responsibility as a child of God. I can no longer leave it to the pastor and staff to do the job the Lord has commanded me to do. The dedicated workers in the training have equipped me and given me the tools to be an effective witness. I hope to spend my remaining years making up for past deficiencies in this area of my Christian walk.

YOU CAN BE A SOUL-WINNING DISCIPLER

How does FAITH work? It works through people who allow Jesus, who lives in them, to do what He wants to do most. The majority of Christians do not allow Christ to have His way through them, especially when it comes to soul winning.

"There was a little city, and a few men within it; and there came a great king against it, and besieged it, and built great bulwarks against it. Now there was found in it a poor wise man, and he by his wisdom delivered the city; yet no man remembered that same poor man" (Eccl. 9:14-15).

One Person! One person seemingly helplessly limited but willing to try! If you will try, Jesus living in you will work miracles.

Not only are we to be soul winners, we are to disciple others and help them to do the same. A soul-winning discipler does two great and glorious things at once. FAITH is based upon just this concept, which is why it is destined to expand not only the number in Sunday School, but the FAITH ministry will expand, also. Additionally, all those involved will grow in

- Bible knowledge,
- prayer ability,
- confidence,
- joy,
- compassion,
- purposefulness, and
- discipline.

In short, they'll grow in Christlikeness because someone has been a soul-winning discipler. That someone should be each of us.

Each of us should be soul-winning disciplers because THE WORLD AROUND US needs Jesus working in, and through, us. The world of Christians needs someone to help them grow. They are a part of our world and part of our responsibility. We should feel obligated to help those newer Christians around us.

You can become a soul-winning discipler not only because there is a world around you that's in need, but because THERE IS A WILL. God has a will for you to become a soul-winning discipler. Jesus has a will for the same. You have the same will because the Lord dwells within you. You do care, and you do want to see people fall in love with Christ and let Him be Lord of their lives.

The reason you have that will is because it is Christ's compassionate heart within you longing to touch those spiritually needy souls around you. Note these verses about Jesus' concern:

> "When he saw the multitudes, he was moved with compassion on them, because they fainted, and were scattered abroad, as sheep having no shepherd" (Matt. 9:36).
>
> "Jesus went forth, and saw a great multitude, and was moved with compassion toward them, and he healed their sick" (Matt. 14:14).

KEY THOUGHTS ON SOUL WINNING

> "Jesus called his disciples unto him, and said, I have compassion on the multitude, because they continue with me now three days, and have nothing to eat: and I will not send them away fasting, lest they faint in the way" (Matt. 15:32).
>
> "Jesus had compassion on them, and touched their eyes: and immediately their eyes received sight, and they followed him" (Matt. 20:34).
>
> "Jesus, moved with compassion, put forth his hand, and touched him, and saith unto him, I will; be thou clean" (Mark 1:41).
>
> "Jesus, when he came out, saw much people, and was moved with compassion toward them, because they were as sheep not having a shepherd: and he began to teach them many things" (Mark 6:34).
>
> "I have compassion on the multitude, because they have now been with me three days, and have nothing to eat" (Mark 8:2).
>
> "When the Lord saw her, he had compassion on her, and said unto her, Weep not" (Luke 7:13).

The Lord Jesus came into this world with the will to give His life for it. Jesus had exactly the same will and compassion every day of His life and work as He did the day He hung on the cross. We are told in Luke 19:41, "He beheld the city, and wept over it." When our mind is allowed to crowd out the lost, our compassionate will to see them won will melt. The obvious way to keep a compassionate will and heart is to stay in close fellowship with Christ.

My systematic, personalized theology has been reduced to one statement. As a boy, I learned quickly in the bitter cold winters an important lesson. The closer you stayed to the heater, the warmer you got, and the farther you got away from the heater, the colder you got. My spiritual conclusion is, "The closer I stay to Jesus, the warmer I get about the things nearest to the heart of God."

People say, "What about this doctrine, what about this program, what about this approach?" My overriding conviction is to do what

Do what you see Jesus

doing in the Bible.

Evangelism Through the Sunday School: A Journey of FAITH

Jesus did. Do what you see Jesus doing in the Bible.

Jesus was a personal soul winner, and He is our example to follow as a personal soul winner. Everywhere Jesus went He was doing soul winning. Look at Him with Nicodemus, "Ye must be born again" (John 3:7) and with the woman at the well (John 4:23-24). See Jesus with the man born blind (John 9:3), with Zacchaeus up in the tree (Luke 19:9), and with the thief on the cross (Luke 23:43). If you follow Jesus and watch Him, you'll discover that He was always doing the work of soul winning.

Jesus not only was the example, Jesus was the exhorter of His disciples to do as He did—win souls.

"Jesus, walking by the sea of Galilee, saw two brethren, Simon called Peter, and Andrew his brother, casting a net into the sea: for they were fishers. And he saith unto them, Follow me, and I will make you fishers of men. And they straightway left their nets, and followed him. And going on from thence, he saw other two brethren, James the son of Zebedee, and John his brother, in a ship with Zebedee their father, mending their nets; and he called them. And they immediately left the ship and their father, and followed him" (Matt. 4:18-22).

That exhortation and call to follow Jesus' example is to all disciples of all time.

You can be a soul-winning discipler because THERE IS A WAY. We know that there is a way because the Lord would never have commanded us to win souls if there was no way to do it. There is a WAY because there is the power to overcome Satan. Here is the key:

KEY THOUGHTS ON SOUL WINNING

> "Go ye therefore, and teach all nations, baptizing them in the name of the Father, and of the Son, and of the Holy Ghost" (Matt. 28:19).
>
> "He shall be great in the sight of the Lord, and shall drink neither wine nor strong drink; and he shall be filled with the Holy Ghost, even from his mother's womb. And many of the children of Israel shall he turn to the Lord their God" (Luke 1:15-16).
>
> "Behold, I send the promise of my Father upon you: but tarry ye in the city of Jerusalem, until ye be endued with power from on high" (Luke 24:49).

> "Ye shall receive power, after that the Holy Ghost is come upon you: and ye shall be witnesses unto me both in Jerusalem, and in all Judaea, and in Samaria, and unto the uttermost part of the earth" (Acts 1:8).
>
> "When they had prayed, the place was shaken where they were assembled together; and they were all filled with the Holy Ghost, and they spake the word of God with boldness" (Acts 4:31).
>
> "He was a good man, and full of the Holy Ghost and of faith: and much people was added unto the Lord" (Acts 11:24).

KEY THOUGHTS ON SOUL WINNING

Throughout this book and the FAITH ministry, it is assumed that the reader understands that the Person who actually does the soul winning is the Lord, through His Holy Spirit. Almost everyone feels comfortable calling Christians "soul winners" if the Christian lets the Holy Spirit win souls to Christ through them. The way to win souls is by the power of God's Holy Spirit, who already is living within you. You can be a soul-winning discipler because you have the power from God.

The first-century Christians believed that fact so earnestly and committed themselves so fully to it that their world was touched by gospel evangelism in a little more than 33 years. The world around us—our world—the 21st century world—waits for us to believe as earnestly and to be as completely committed as those early christians.

There is a WAY because of the WORD OF GOD.

> "I am not ashamed of the gospel of Christ: for it is the power of God unto salvation to every one that believeth; to the Jew first, and also to the Greek" (Rom. 1:16).
>
> "Being born again, not of corruptible seed, but of incorruptible, by the word of God, which liveth and abideth for ever" (1 Pet. 1:23).
>
> "The law of the Lord is perfect, converting the soul: the testimony of the Lord is sure, making wise the simple" (Ps. 19:7).

Evangelism Through the Sunday School: A Journey of FAITH

Paul made it clear in 1 Corinthians 2:1 that we are not to go out attempting to persuade people to Christ "with excellency of speech or of wisdom, declaring unto you the testimony of God." No, we must rely upon the power of God's Spirit and God's Scripture. They are powerful to the tearing down of strongholds, defeating the devil, and winning souls. The Bible likens itself to a sword: "The word of God is quick, and powerful, and sharper than any two-edged sword, piercing even to the dividing asunder of soul and spirit, and of the joints and marrow, and is a discerner of the thoughts and intents of the heart" (Heb. 4:12).

The Word of God is loaded with supernatural power. God's Word has the power to go like a sword into a person's heart, soul, and spirit to convict and convert. You have the power of God's Word where you are and with it, you can become a soul-winning discipler!

There is a WAY because there is the FAITH ministry. The FAITH approach is developed upon a biblical foundation and the New Testament type of training. It enjoys spiritual results that can be identified in the early church's life. True, Paul and our forefathers of the faith did not have today's book, notebook, and materials, as does the FAITH Sunday School evangelism ministry. They did, however, have in their hearts precisely what FAITH has at its heart and what FAITH implants into the hearts of those who use it.

The Word of God is like a sword, but a sword works best when the holder knows how to use it. The Holy Spirit is like electricity, but the Spirit works best when there is a directed conduit. That is what the FAITH ministry is all about. It is a tried, proven, and well-refined way to help Christians understand that way and be used of the Lord, His Word, and His Spirit to do soul winning and discipling.

People usually first see FAITH as a way to carry out the Great Commission and win souls. That is a prominent result. That holy result is, however, the outcome of some other things that first take place. FAITH begins at the point of the person who is a Christian. Its aim is to, by the Grace of God, build great Christians. In turn, great Christians will build great churches. Then, great churches without fail will carry out as a number-one priority their Great Commission. (If a church fails the latter, it cannot be considered a Great Commission church by New Testament standards. Furthermore, it has failed its members because they've not been discipled to be New Testament, Great Commission Christians.)

FAITH starts with a willing person and goes around the world with the cause of Christ! What a trip for all those saints in the Sunday School! I spoke with a woman about 70 years of age, saying, "When you and your husband walked down the aisle of this church, did you ever expect that you would be going to Honduras on a mission trip?" She replied, "Never in a million years, but I'm ready to go again tomorrow!" You may be certain that when the FAITH ministry brings a person to such spiritual commitment, that person will not be reluctant to become a soul-winning discipler.

Any Christian can become a soul-winning discipler because there is THE WORLD, A WILL, A WAY, and THE WORD.

FAITH is the ministry that any church of any size can use, through its Sunday School, to bring people to Jesus because that church's leaders and laypeople become soul-winning disciplers.

MARK S. HAWKS

MEDIAN ADULT 1
SUNDAY SCHOOL
CLASS

COMPUTER
SPECIALIST

All Comes Together

Sunday School evangelism training is teaching me how to share my faith with others and how to put my beliefs into a language that is easy for others to understand. It has increased my biblical base of knowledge, which makes it easier for me to talk with authority about God's Word. I think that the most important lesson I have learned so far is the overview of how God's plan for salvation works. I have been aware of the individual points expressed, but the way they fit together to form a complete idea was new to me. It is like seeing a great piece of artwork that you have been getting glimpses of suddenly completely uncovered.

AVOID THE NO-WIN COLLISION COURSE

The Sunday School organization and an aggressive evangelism training ministry tend to be on a collision course. Because the Sunday School is the largest organization in the church, it most likely will be the survivor following the collision. Here is what is meant by a "collision course" and why it will happen.

Let's say that Jim is an attender or perhaps the teacher of a median adult men's Sunday School class. Jim feels and understands the need to be enrolled in the evangelism training ministry of his church. Jim's evangelism training team is comprised of a young adult and a single adult. Each team member is from a different Sunday School age group and class. That means that likely their daily lives and family circumstances also are different.

Each week, as Jim receives the team's visitation assignments, he finds that he rarely is visiting median adults who are the age for his Sunday School class. Jim correctly feels a need and desire to help his class to minister to its members and to reach those who are prospects for his age group and class. Jim is frustrated because he does not have time to visit the prospects for his class and does not have time to make ministry visits that some of the class members need. He is beginning to feel that his evangelism ministry involvement is preventing him from carrying out his obligations to his class. Jim decides not to participate in the evangelism ministry any longer.

Too bad for Jim, his class, the lost, his evangelism partners, and his church, because collision has occurred and the evangelism ministry is the casualty. After a series of such drop outs, one can imagine what happens to the evangelism ministry. In such a collision, no one really wins except Satan. The Sunday School does not reach its potential. The lost continue to die and go to hell. Baptism and attendance remain about the same. The Sunday School and church continue to move along at the same slow pace of enthusiasm and growth as before. It really is a no-win collision that must be avoided and can be avoided because the solution to such a situation is right at the heart of FAITH. The collision is not inevitable. It can be averted, and FAITH will bring the two efforts together on a mutual course toward the same worthy goals that grow and bless the people. What usually is a collision will become a powerful connection as Sunday School and evangelism combine to become a divine duo working for the Lord.

FAITH is the ministry that any church of any size can use.

"BUT WAIT! I DON'T HAVE THE GIFT OF EVANGELISM!"

The clear goal of God, the Commission of Christ, and the command to the church is that every believer is to be doing soul-winning witnessing. Soul-winning witnessing is to become a way of life and is to continue.

Nowhere in the Holy Scriptures is the church encouraged to discover a small group of specialized members to go out and do the work of soul winning on behalf of the remainder of the membership. No biblically oriented church would do that any more than they would attempt to discover a small group of rich people among their membership to do the giving on behalf of the entire congregation. Every member has commands in regard to financial stewardship, and no one can obey for another. Individuals are responsible before God to obey God's instructions concerning their own financial stewardship.

That is what occurs much of the time in a church when it comes to soul-winning evangelism. A small group is singled out to do soul winning for the entire church while the vast majority concerns itself very little with their Great Commission obligation. Those people busy themselves with church work that is centered on nurturing and growth.

Be assured that I am committed to Christian and church efforts at nurturing and growing as much as I am to evangelism. But, churches are not to fall into any ministry approach that encourages the follower of Christ away from their individual commission, command, and obligation to be personally involved in soul-winning evangelism.

One of the things that has contributed to a church and its members leaving soul winning to only a few people is the widely publicized misunderstanding about what is called the "spiritual gift of evangelism."

Although most Christians have heard much about or read books promoting the "spiritual gift of evangelism," that term or teaching as such is not found in the Bible. That term and teaching is not listed among the lists of spiritual gifts found in 1 Corinthians 12:8-10, 1 Corinthians 12:28-30, and Romans 12:6-8.

Usually, the one verse that is taken out of context to authenticate such a position is Ephesians 4:11, where Paul wrote not of gifts: "He gave some, apostles; and some, prophets; and some, evangelists; and some, pastors and teachers." The context, according to many Bible scholars, has to do with the leadership positions, or offices, of the church for the purpose of training members to serve and minister. Evangelists were men who traveled across the country from church to church in areas where the faith had not yet been proclaimed. They would equip Christians for ministry. They purposed to work with pastors and teachers at a church and then move on. The title was given to Philip (Acts 21:8). Timothy was charged to "do the work of an evangelist" (2 Tim. 4:5). Epaphras, of whom Paul wrote in Colossians 1:7, no doubt was in this category.

I do not see that this calling can be correctly interpreted as a spiritual gift of evangelism among only some of the members of today's church.

When only a few people understand that they have, and thus practice, the spiritual gift of evangelism, the soul-winning work force is greatly diminished. When such concepts as that of relationship evangelism hold sway in a church, months or even years go by before lost people receive a soul-winning witness.

The failure of most relationship evangelism today is that it is 99 percent relationship and little evangelism. Two reasons: (1) People who feel they don't have the "gift of evangelism" don't sense any real obligation to win souls. (2) Usually the person does not know how to win anyone to Christ because there has been no need to learn. Other members supposedly have the "gift" of evangelism and thus are the ones counted upon to do soul winning.

This foolish focus on evangelism has been convenient and acceptable to our western world culture and enjoyed by both leaders and laypeople in the church. Regrettably, the approach is hurting our churches, denying participation to our members, and disregarding God's command. At the same time, a lost and dying world goes straight to hell.

I've read that some of the leading "experts" have said that those who are not in the 5-10 percent of members responsible for evangelism should in no way feel blame or guilt about the lack of soul-winning evangelism. I would like to ask:

Who do we think will feel the blame and guilt when our churches and communities are abandoned to the world?

Who do we think will feel the blame and guilt when our families and friends die without any assurance of salvation and heaven?

Who do we think will feel the blame and guilt when heaven is robbed and hell fills up with the souls our generation should have won?

Who do we think will feel the blame and guilt when God/Christ ask each of us about our responsibility to witness and win our world in our lifetime?

You may disagree with my personal conviction that there is no spiritual "gift of evangelism," but it is not possible to disagree with the biblical imperative that every Christian is to be a soul winner actively carrying out Jesus' Great Commission.

EVANGELISM: PRIORITY ONE

The effective evangelistic church has a philosophy of ministry with evangelism at its core because soul winning was Christ's number one command for the church.

> Luke 19:10: "The Son of man is come to seek and to save that which was lost."
>
> Matthew 20:28: "The Son of man came not to be ministered unto, but to minister, and to give his life a ransom for many."
>
> I Timothy 1:15: "This is a faithful saying, and worthy of acceptation, that Christ Jesus came into the world to save sinners."

The church of the first century knew nothing of a specialized few to do the work of winning their world. They all entered into the glorious enterprise of colaboring with God to win souls.

Jesus' apostles and the early church members took Him seriously. They taught people publicly and from house to house. They testified for Christ, both to the Jews and to the Gentiles. They took the good news of the truth in Christ to all the known world. Christian history reveals that since apostolic times, wherever the church has maintained an evangelistic missionary zeal and a soul-winning fervor, the Holy Spirit of God has given his blessings. Wherever the church has lost its missionary zeal and soul-winning fervor, God has moved on.

Billy Graham frequently has said that the chief duty and privilege of the Christian is soul winning. Scripture says, "He which converteth the sinner from the error of his way shall save a soul from death, and shall hide a multitude of sins" (Jas. 5:20).

There are many preachers but few soul winners. There are many books of sermons but few on soul winning. Perhaps the neglect of the Christian's prime business is one of the causes for the church's failure to lead more men and women to Christ. Even so, such men as John Wesley, David Brainerd, and Stephen Olford taught the primacy of soul winning by all Christians. Thus, the motto and mission of every local church should be EVERY MEMBER EVANGELISM. The words of our commission by Jesus have never been withdrawn, and the vision for world evangelization is still as clear as when He first presented it.

Example from the Battlefield

My first mission in Vietnam as a scout platoon leader was to track down about 300 enemy soldiers, using as a guide a wounded enemy prisoner. My commanding officer said, "Those are your orders." I had only 28 men, so the odds did not look good for my first mission!

I will never forget the relief I felt when over my radio came a second set of orders to supersede the first: "Mission cancelled." Whew! Our platoon began to loosen our equipment, lay our weapons aside, and relax. That's the way you do when superseding orders cancel your mission.

From the way many of us act, it appears that we have heard some superseding orders that counteract our Great Commission from God. If you have got such an idea, it did not come from God.

There are two quotations from Christ that always should be linked together: "The Son of man is come to seek and to save that which was lost" (Luke 19:10) and "As my Father hath sent me, even so send I you" (John 20:21). Those two revelations of the divine direction are inseparably related.

When Jesus was standing on the Mount of Olives before His ascension, His last command was regarding the Christian's duty to witness to lost people (Acts 1:8). He promised to direct His disciples where and to whom they should bear witness. The early disciples took that command. They never ceased trying. Their passion for souls was kept aflame by constant spiritual fellowship with Christ and also by their efforts to win others.

The church and leaders today are accountable before God to motivate, train, equip, and encourage every Christian member to be a soul-winning witness. FAITH is the best and most appropriate way to do that, and the effort is best made through the Sunday School.

There are many preachers but few soul winners. There are many books of sermons but few on soul winning.

DON BRAGG

SINGLE ADULT 4
SUNDAY SCHOOL
DIRECTOR

TRAVEL AGENT

Easily Discouraged

When I joined the Sunday School evangelism training, I came into it as one who was discouraged because the witnessing ways I had used before did not work. I found the training to be an organized, disciplined approach to the gospel presentation that is simple to understand and easy to present. I thank the Lord for giving me this opportunity. I am glad to have competent, trained individuals giving of their time to help me be a better witness for the Lord.

PENNY SCOTT

MEDIAN ADULT 4
SUNDAY SCHOOL
CLASS

MIDDLE SCHOOL
PUBLIC SCHOOL
TEACHER

If Anyone Would Ask

I first heard of Sunday School evangelism training before we were members of First Baptist, Daytona Beach. It certainly sounded like a good idea for people who had the time. I didn't want to offend anyone and thought I had an equally good plan. I was ready to share my faith IF ANYONE WOULD ASK ME. Now that I look back, I realize how lame an effort that was. Did I expect that I would be sitting on the beach or eating lunch at a restaurant and someone would approach me and ask for my testimony? Big surprise! It never happened.

When I find a store having a big sale, I call my fiends and relatives and tell them the good news. I want them to be able to get in on the good bargains. What does that say about me and my priorities? Don't I want people to find out how to have eternal life? I do now!

VISITATION—THE WAY IT USUALLY IS

It usually goes like this: A team of people go out from the church to visit. The age and interest of those on the visiting team have little in common with those they are going to visit or with each other. The team is invited into a Sunday School prospect's home and finds that the prospect is not a Christian. The team is not equipped or encouraged to do more than invite lost people to church and Sunday School. The visiting team later will attempt to get someone on the staff or a trained soul winner to go to that home.

Another predicament is when the church has a group of trained soul winners who go out visiting. They are not together based upon age, interest, or Sunday School class. This soul-winning team goes to a home of a recent church visitor. The person the team visits is not the age of anyone on the team, and it is discovered that the person already is a Christian but hasn't decided to join the team's church. The visiting soul-winning team will try to get someone to visit who can meet the needs of this person.

Neither of those two hypothetical visitation teams are composed of bad-intended people. They are doing what they were sent to do, and they usually do it in the ways just described. It can be done so much more sensibly, effectively, and rewardingly!

VISITATION—THE WAY IT COULD BE

A FAITH Team is composed of three people who have in common a Sunday School group and age group. This team is equipped not only to do a Sunday School visit for members or prospective members, but also to do soul-winning visits. Consequently, there is no reason to waste time and opportunities by deferring needs to a later date and to other people.

When a FAITH Team visits, it will call on people in the same Sunday School age group as that of the team. Should the prospect not be a Christian, the FAITH Team can effectively and warmly present the gospel as they have been trained. Should this person pray to accept Christ, this same team is able to continue with immediate follow-up actions that include public confession and enrollment in their Sunday School class and/or department. One or more persons on the team will arrange to meet and welcome this new friend to church and Sunday School the next week .

Should it be discovered that the prospect already is a Christian but has needs particular to this age group, the team is prepared to have such a ministering encounter.

The FAITH Team will be able to identify and help with the needs as they have been trained. They can encourage the prospect to come and meet with them and some others in the Sunday School class. The FAITH Team is competent to enroll this person in their own Sunday School class and department and meet, greet, and welcome this new friend into their group. The person is to be invited and made to feel welcome at other events.

HERE'S HOW FAITH WORKS

This portion is an overview, so I will generalize. It is presented for the sake of disclosing the overall scope and flow of The FAITH SUNDAY SCHOOL EVANGELISM MINISTRY in relationship to your church.

FAITH is most concisely understood under three broad headings:

I. FOUNDATION—BIBLICAL

Biblical refers to several scriptural convictions shared by evangelical Christians.

A. "Seek and Save." Jesus came to this earth and gave His life for this purpose, notably. (John 3:16, Luke 19:10, and Matt. 20:28).

B. "Go Into All The World." Jesus' great commandment to each of us is GO—WIN—DISCIPLE the world.

C. "Ye are a chosen generation, a royal priesthood, an holy nation, a peculiar people; that ye should shew forth the praises of him who hath called you out of darkness into his marvellous light: Which in time past were not a people, but are not the people of God: which had not obtained mercy, but now have obtained mercy" (1 Pet. 2:9-10). The church is the collected saints in a unified desire and effort to do what Jesus did and what Jesus told us to do.

D. "Go-Disciple-Baptize-Teach" (Matt. 28:19-20). Sunday School is the expression of the biblical model to go out, win people, and come together to study and learn.

The Sunday School can bring more people in the shortest amount of time to do the most worthwhile work over the longest period than any other group in the church. That requires organization and New Testament style training about New Testament teachings. Sunday School provides such an organization, but the training needs to be added.

"The things that thou hast heard of me among many witnesses, the same commit thou to faithful men, who shall be able to teach others also" (2 Tim. 2:2).

To be "able to teach others" requires training. There then must be a way to pass those things learned on to others. FAITH training will do just that. This discipling atmosphere is fostered by the learning-training structure that you can easily trace in the following events.

Originator Clinic. The first training clinic where the FAITH approach of First Baptist, Daytona Beach, was transferred to other churches and their Sunday Schools was called the Originator Clinic. Churches that attended the Originator Clinic became the initial Trainer Churches.

Training Clinics. Churches that desire FAITH training will attend a Training Clinic and receive everything needed to implement a successful FAITH ministry in their own Sunday School and church. Upon completion of the Training Clinic, the new churches will be qualified to pass on the training to their Sunday School members. These churches are now considered to be FAITH Churches.

FAITH Training in the Church. This effort is encouraged and promoted to the members of the Sunday School of the FAITH CHURCHES returning from their learning time at a TRAINING CLINIC. Participants have learned and are now able to teach others and will do so to their members of the Sunday School.

FAITH Facilitator. The person in the FAITH CHURCH who will do the training during the class phase, with at least one classroom teacher. An assistant teacher for each class is helpful.

Team Training. This type of leadership is the connection of three people linked together in accountability, friendship, and discipleship. They are together for the aim of training and learning in the on-the-job phase. The Team Leader will lead his/her team to learn the FAITH approach of ministering to both members of the Sunday School and those who are prospects for the Sunday School. They will learn both nurturing and evangelism.

Team Leader. This is the leader and teacher during the on-the-job phase of each week's training. There is a sense of concern and care by the FAITH Team Leader for the other two members on the team related to their common spiritual growth experience.

Learner. This is a beginner in the FAITH ministry. During the early years of FAITH, there usually will be two such persons on each team. After a few years of FAITH, a team sometimes will have an assistant team leader along with only one trainee. Assistant team leaders have team leader skills or are approaching the time when they will train but presently may be needed as the third member to complete a team.

Encourager. This is a person who has completed training. This person seems to be best suited as a "silent" Team member. This person is, however, an excellent connector of the focus Sunday School class to the person being visited.

You may say, "That surely is organized and committed training and learning." You are correct, and the beauty is that it is done by laypeople and works beautifully while building great Christians who build great churches that carry out the Great Commission!

III. RESULTS—SPIRITUAL

Spiritual results are the only outcome anticipated if a FAITH ministry is biblically founded and directed by New Testament training to disciple members of the Sunday School "for the work of the ministry" (Eph. 4:12). That is what FAITH will produce without fail.

For the sake of saving time and space and avoiding repetition, let me call upon you to review what was noted in Part 2: "Results You Can Expect" and "Four Areas of Results."

THE MOST IMPORTANT LINK

When the FAITH ministry is established and advances as suggested, it will produce the desired expectations. There are yet two other things that make FAITH work. They are what I call (1) THE MOST IMPORTANT LINK and (2) THE KEY INGREDIENT.

THE MOST IMPORTANT LINK is that the inseparable golden link that maintains the union of Sunday School and evangelism training is that of the two weekly leadership meetings. Both of those important gatherings constitute the "bonding agent" for a successful FAITH ministry. The "how to" of each is fully taught at the FAITH Training Clinics. Here is a sketch of each weekly leadership meeting.

Sunday School Leaders must meet each week. FAITH makes the weekly meeting people-centered, and a new excitement is generated upon combining Sunday School and evangelism. When FAITH

Evangelism Through the Sunday School: A Journey of FAITH

begins in your church and you do the things you learn at the Training Clinic, the weekly meeting will come alive and grow. Your training manual received at the clinic will ensure good results.

FAITH Group Leader Meeting occurs each week. This meeting is in addition to the Sunday School Leaders Meeting. This group's size will vary, depending on the number of people in your evangelism training effort. Every Sunday School Division should have at least one FAITH Group Leader. FAITH Group Leaders are the people who are responsible to ensure the best training and visitation assignments. FAITH Group Leaders form one important section of the accountability network woven into FAITH.

Both meetings deal with ministry visits for those already in Sunday School and also prospects who are not in Sunday School, some of whom are unsaved people. The Sunday School Leaders Meeting once a week primarily deals with Sunday School but has a strong evangelism influence. The Group Leader Meeting once a week primarily deals with evangelism but has a strong Sunday School influence.

THE KEY INGREDIENT to all the training, learning, growing, going, winning, and discipling through FAITH in any Sunday School and church is Commitment. FAITH works well for those who are deeply committed to the Great Commission.

Our church has had the privilege of training hundreds of pastors and laypeople outside of our church from across the nation and around the world. Each time we have had a Training Clinic, we have invited attendees to comment on their training/learning experience. The one thing always highlighted is the commitment of our Sunday School laypeople.

The visiting church leaders have been quick to recognize the "key ingredient" of commitment in the laypeople. So many of those church and denominational leaders have gone home and discovered that their laypeople were exactly the same as ours. All they needed was leadership in commitment and a ministry like FAITH through which to develop.

Isn't it a wonderful accomplishment when laypeople of your church's Sunday School now are leading and training, not only their fellow members but pastors, staff, missionaries and others from around the world? Disciples exchanging and transferring biblical truths as they go along their life's journey in Jesus. That's New

Testament training. You might say, "I'm not sure our church's laypeople can do that." I will absolutely guarantee you that many of them can do just as well or better than ours can do. But you have to believe in them and the Christ that indwells them. "I can do all things through Christ which strengtheneth me." (Phil. 4:13). The people must have a way to be motivated to train and learn. Your example of commitment and FAITH will be what they need!

How does it work? It works great and in direct proportion to the commitment exemplified through leadership, which is then caught by all those who train and learn through FAITH. It can happen, it waits to happen, it will happen, if someone like you will be courageous and try.

HOW DO WE KEEP IT GOING?

"I believe I understand how FAITH works, but how does it keep going year after year?

That is an experienced, insightful, and fair question. Many ministries and programs are designed to last only a short time. FAITH is not a "quick fix," but a long-haul approach that becomes more productive with time. Because of its long period of development and 12 years of intense testing and piloting, FAITH is constructed to continue for years on an increasingly productive course without any devastating surprises.

The short answer to the question "How do we keep it going strong?" would be to say, "Implement FAITH just as you are taught at the Training Clinic." I have listed items that will keep it going strongly. As you read them, you'll be convinced of these two important facts. One, FAITH is committed to the long haul. Two, FAITH material already has identified and solved for your church those areas that have potential to weaken your ministry. Local church leaders will be wise to use this list to evaluate how FAITH is being conducted in their church.

FAITH is not a "quick fix."

1. Pastor/Staff continue to
   A. Participate actively and openly
   B. Promote actively and openly
2. Start Correctly
   A. Prepare for involvement in a training clinic
   B. Participate in a Training Clinic
3. Enrollment Methods (use all three)
   A. Individual one-to-one

B. Congregation "All on the Altar"

C. Enrollment Banquet

4. Follow Training Model

   A. Class Time and Schedule

   B. Materials Used

5. Commit to ongoing training (at least two STEPS per year)

6. Teach People to Love Fishing (not just catching)

7. "Good" Visits must be experienced by teams

8. Sunday School ministry visits must be provided and encouraged

9. Train and Visit at the same time, night or day

10. Leadership Meetings

    A. Sunday School Leaders

    B. FAITH Group Leaders

11. Danger Zones must be recognized

12. Sunday School connected in every way

13. Recognition Service

If FAITH is conducted in a local church, following the model practiced and taught at Training Clinics, which includes the list of suggested items to keep the program going, it is destined to become even stronger year after year. You'll have little difficulty keeping it going.

THE PERSON GOD USES

I found a book years ago while on a mission trip in the West Indies. It was an old paperback, dog-eared, almost-worn-out copy of Oswald J. Smith's book *The Man God Uses*. It didn't look like much, but it was gold to me and changed my life forever! Do your best to find a copy, then read it. I wrote in the front of my copy of the book, "I am praying to become and be a person that God uses!" It has become apparent to me that many of the things God favors, blesses, and uses in a person can be understood by reading Acts 6:1-5.

While there is a specific purpose for those in the passage, it pictures THE PERSON GOD USES. The godly characteristics in Acts 6 apply to all of Christian life, but for the soul-winning discipler in FAITH, they make a notable difference. Each time I've had a dry spell in witnessing or have felt a strong move of the devil against me, I have gone to that passage to recheck my personal spiritual life. Perhaps the passage will help you not only to be THE PERSON GOD USES but to serve as your spiritual inventory checklist.

Here is the list of Christian characteristics gleaned from Acts 6:1-5:

1. A SAVED PERSON. "Among you" (v. 3) signifies that the people God was going to use were Christians. THE PERSON GOD USES to do soul winning is to be a saved person, a born-again soul with a personal relationship to Jesus Christ as Savior and Lord.

"The natural man receiveth not the things of the Spirit of God: for they are foolishness unto him: nor can he know them, because they are spiritually discerned" (1 Cor. 2:14).

BECKY DARBY

**MEDIAN ADULT 3
SUNDAY SCHOOL
CLASS**

**INTERNATIONAL
SPEEDWAY
CORPORATION**

Fears Gone

Some of the women in my Sunday School Class would occasionally mention Sunday School Evangelism Training and how it had helped them in witnessing. I needed to know how to share my faith.

The nerves really set in when I discovered that I would be involved in visiting homes to present the gospel. I discovered that others were nervous, but the overall attitude was enthusiasm in spite of people's fears. I thought I'd never be able to learn all that material. Furthermore, the 16 weeks was an intimidating length of time!

It turned out that through the study, the Scriptures, the practice, the accountability, and the example of the trainers, the "big picture" began to take shape, and my concern for others' salvation began to grow.

What I feel I have gained through this program is a much greater sense of how many people don't know Christ and a much greater concern for those who don't. I have an awareness that I am more usable by God and more ready and able to share His love.

The unsaved person has no power with God, no discernment of spiritual happenings, no confidence nor experience in what they are attempting to share. "Without faith it is impossible to please him" (Heb. 11:6).

The saved person needs to be assured of his or her own salvation. If you are in doubt about your salvation, you should just stop reading and tell Jesus you thank Him for keeping you alive to this moment and that you are stating your belief in His death, burial, and resurrection. You are turning from your self and your sin to His forgiveness. You trust in Jesus and Him alone for your salvation.

THE PEOPLE GOD USES are saved and secure people.

2. A SELECTED PERSON. "Look ye out" (v. 3) denotes that God was searching for people to use throughout the body of believers. THE PERSON GOD USES will be a member of a local church. Don't make the foolish mistake of trying to "spiritualize" away the local church. Someone has said that claiming to be a Christian without being an active, committed church member is like:

- A student who will not go to school
- A soldier who will not join the army
- A citizen who does not pay taxes or vote
- A salesman with no customers
- An explorer with no base camp
- A seaman on a ship without a crew
- A businessman on a deserted island
- An author without readers
- A tuba player without an orchestra
- A parent without a family
- A football player without a team
- A politician who is a hermit
- A scientist who does not share his findings
- A bee without a hive

There is nowhere on earth a better place to grow in Christ than the local church. I heard of a group discussion among some church members. One said, "I can't remember the content of any sermon in the past 10 years, and I've heard them all!" Another person concluded, "What's the use of going to church if we can't remember what we've heard? Maybe we can use our time better in another way!" Then, a lady of the group put the statements in perspective: "I have eaten 30,000 meals or more, and I can't remember them. But I know this. If I had not had those meals, I'd be dead today!"

The PERSON GOD USES will be an active member of a local church.

SEPARATED

She's correct because so much of what happens that is good in our local church goes unnoticed yet is vital to our spiritual life. THE PERSON GOD USES will be an active member of a local church. That active membership is to include Sunday School. I've said over and over that if a person must choose between worship service and Sunday School, I will tell them to go to Sunday School, because there is where one makes vital friendship relations, has the fellowship the way godly people should, and becomes part of a care and keeping network.

In the INVITATION PORTION of the FAITH Outline process, one does not spend much time trying to show people how to grow in Christ at home with a spiritual "Do-It-Yourself" kit. Rather, the time is used to bring the person to a personal connection with the local church and Sunday School where it is believed that the individual is able to grow correctly and survive spiritually. Any experienced church person will accept readily FAITH's three-step approach to moving a person from home into the caring embrace of the local church and Sunday School. FAITH closes the gap between the person and the local church.

The PERSON GOD USES will be an active member of a local church.

3. A SEPARATED PERSON. "Out" (v. 3) seems to denote that the person God plans to use is to be separated. Never has there been a day like today that the lost world needed to see a difference between their sinful lives and the Christian life.

No matter how much rationalization is offered, the world expects Christians to be different. They have every right to expect that because *different* is a biblical characteristic of THE PERSON GOD USES. The call of God to His people to be separated continues to this day. "Come out from among them, and be ye separate, saith the Lord" (2 Cor. 6:17) and "Be ye not unequally yoked together with the unbelievers" (2 Cor. 6:14).

If we desire God to use us, we will continually wage war to be separated from sin and selfishness. Further, we will be separated unto our Savior, Jesus. Not only are we separated from sin, but we are to be separated to Jesus.

Since mine eyes were fixed on Jesus,
I've lost sight of all besides,
So enchained my spirit's vision,
 Looking at the Crucified.
  (Author Unknown)
THE PERSON GOD USES is a separated person.

Evangelism Through the Sunday School: A Journey of FAITH

4. A SOUND PERSON. "Honest report" (v. 3) has a lot to say about reputation. THE PERSON GOD USES will have a reputation as a Christian who is humble and lives by the Word of God.

> Matthew 18:4: "Whosoever therefore shall humble himself as this little child, the same is the greatest in the kingdom of heaven."
>
> Matthew 5:3: "Blessed are the poor in spirit: for theirs is the kingdom of heaven."
>
> Luke 10:20: "Not withstanding in this rejoice not, that the spirits are subject unto you; but rather rejoice, because your names are written in heaven."

Humility is understanding who God is and who we are and then going about living our daily lives showing that we understand those facts! Humility does not mean spiritlessness, weakness, cowardliness, or an inferiority complex. It means a life of high spiritual courage and strength. Humility is meekness.

For THE PERSON GOD USES, there is one scriptural action required: we are "to humble ourselves" (Luke 18:14; 14:11; Matt. 23:12; 18:4; 2 Chron. 7:14; 33:12, 1 Pet. 5:5).

If we refuse to "humble ourselves," there are several predictable consequences. (1) God Himself can humble us (Matt. 3:12; Luke 18:14; 14:11; Matt. 18:4). (2) God can allow others to humble us (2 Chron. 33:11-13). (3) God can allow us to destroy ourselves because of a lack or loss of humility. Samson (Judg. 13:1—16:31) is a clear example of how pride takes the place of humility and leads to destruction. (4) God can allow us to go unhumbled and unused. This result may be the saddest of all. THE PERSON GOD USES will humble himself or herself.

5. A SPIRITUAL PERSON. "Full of the Holy Ghost" (v. 3) says that God is looking to use people who are full of the Holy Spirit. The first qualification for people used by God is not popularity, seniority, or ability. It is our spiritual walk with Jesus by the power of His Spirit. God wants to use people who will allow Him to control their lives by His Holy Spirit.

My understanding and experience with the Bible and the Spirit on this subject is that having the fullness of the Holy Spirit is His having complete control of your life. God wants to accomplish His mission through Spirit-filled people. The outcome of the Spirit is recorded in Galatians 5:22-23.

Being spiritual presupposes a committed prayer life. It is possible to get things done through Spirit-filled praying when nothing else will work.

THE PERSON GOD USES believes that God can do all and will do all through a Spirit-filled vessel.

6 . A SENSITIVE PERSON. "Full of ... wisdom" (v. 3) alerts us that God uses a person who is discerning to His Will and has spiritual insight. How to obtain that is found in James 1:5 and 3:13-18. Persons who are sensitive to the heart of God will see the needs people have. The concern of God is the spiritual welfare of people, especially the spiritual lostness that is a person's eternal death sentence. When Jesus and the Father have their way in us, we will reflect the same concern for lost people. "When he saw the multitudes, he was moved with compassion on them, because they fainted and were scattered abroad, as sheep having no shepherd. Then saith he unto his disciples, The harvest truly is plenteous, but the labourers are few. Pray ye therefore the Lord of the harvest will send forth labourers into his Harvest" (Matt. 9:36-38).

The way of God's intercession through us follows the path of exposure, burden, prayer, participation, and cost. First, we get exposed. "Lift up your eyes" (John 4:35). Then, we become burdened with "great heaviness and continual sorrow" (Rom. 9:2). Next, we'll pray and talk with the Lord, and He'll talk to us about our need to do something. After that, we'll become participants in His work of intercession. And, of course, there always will be times of sacrifice or inconvenience, but the rewards will abundantly outweigh the cost. God is debtor to no man, and what a thrill it is to be a colaborer with God!

THE PERSON GOD USES is sensitive to God's will and call.

7. A STEADFAST PERSON. "Full of faith" (v. 5) says that a believer is faithful to trust the Lord.

Willingness to try to be what Jesus wants is a certain indicator of humble trust in the Lord. The boy with the loaves and fishes (John 6:8-13) is a perfect example of how an unknown person trusted Jesus with what he had and God worked a miracle through his gift. I've always tried to pray that in my life I will be willing to be like the little night-light down at the end of the hallway that is faithfully there all the time, willing to be used. It is so easy to get the idea that we should be a huge, ornate chandelier in the main room.

> "Because the foolishness of God is wiser than men; and the weakness of God is stronger than men. For ye see your calling, brethren, how not many wise men after the flesh, not many mighty, not many noble, are called. But God has chosen the foolish things of the world to confound the wise, and God has chosen the weak things of the world to confound the things which are mighty. … That no flesh should glory in his presence" (1 Cor. 1:25-27, 29).

God will so use unlikely and ordinary persons if they are willing. Consider how God reached Naaman through "a little maid" (2 Kings 5:2). God used Ananias to lead Paul (Acts 9:10-18). The Bible is full of how God uses faithful, willing, ordinary folk. Today, God still is using people like you and me to touch and change lives through His grace if we'll allow Him.

When you find a steadfast, faithful, willing person, you usually will find a person who is disciplined and has a plan. The FAITH ministry helps willing people to develop a systematic approach to growing in Christlikeness and in witnessing to the world.

THE PERSON GOD USES is steadfast and willing.

8. A SERVANT PERSON. "This business" (v. 3) was the serving business. What great company you will be in when you are numbered among the servants! "It shall not be so among you: but whosoever will be great among you, let him be your minister; And whosoever will be chief among you, let him be your servant: Even as the Son of Man came not to be ministered unto, but to minister, and to give his life a ransom for many" (Matt. 20:26-28).

Jesus said in that text that becoming a servant is where real greatness lies with Him and in the kingdom to come. In Philippians 2:5-11, God said that His Son became a servant in His earthly ministry. Paul did what Jesus did and what Jesus tells us to do. (See 1 Cor. 9:19.) In 1 Corinthians 7:20-24, the Bible says that if we want to be used of God, we are to continue in serving the Lord as a servant.

So, servanthood is a holy place. It is the place where God and Christ desire each of us to live out our earthly existence. It is the place of great usefulness and great blessings for here and for eternity!

SERVANT

> "Take heed unto thyself."
> 1 Timothy 4:16
>
> "They made me the keeper of the vineyards;
> but my own vineyard have I not kept."
> Song of Solomon 1:6

THE PERSON GOD USES CHECKLIST

- ☑ 1. I know I am saved.
- ☑ 2. I have assurance of my salvation.
- ☑ 3. I have followed Christ in scriptural baptism.
- ☑ 4. I am active in Sunday School and church.
- ☑ 5. I am living a separated life.
- ☑ 6. I am praying for God to use me.
- ☑ 7. I am spending time in God's Word.
- ☑ 8. I am encouraging others.
- ☑ 9. I have forgiven others.
- ☑ 10. I have asked forgiveness from others.
- ☑ 11. I am endeavoring to humble myself.
- ☑ 12. I am giving glory to God.
- ☑ 13. I am yielding to Jesus' control.
- ☑ 14. I have a consistent prayer life.
- ☑ 15. I am living the servant life.
- ☑ 16. I have several unsaved people on my heart.
- ☑ 17. I am making much of Jesus.
- ☑ 18. I am trying to help another Christian to grow.
- ☑ 19. I am not committing any known sin.
- ☑ 20. I am verbally trying to win others to Christ.
- ☑ 21. I have a definite ministry in my church.

PART 4

How Do I Get FAITH Training?

Training Clinics

EQUIP AND PREPARE CHURCHES

TO EFFECTIVELY USE FAITH

SUNDAY SCHOOL EVANGELISM TRAINING.

BUSY LAYPEOPLE RUN TO FAITH

It was about 5:30 p.m., and I had just finished hospital visitation and was making my way to the car through the drizzling rain. I clearly recognized a friend jogging from the hospital across the parking lot to his office on the other side of the street. He was a member of our church. He also was the chief of staff of the hospital.

"Hey, Doc, I called out." Although it was obvious he recognized me, he hardly acknowledged me and never slowed his pace. His response was totally unlike his friendly, outgoing character.

Man, that sure is strange, I thought. Was it the rain, an emergency, a bad day? Had someone made him angry, or what?

I made my way back to the church where the crowd had begun assembling for supper, to be followed by classroom teaching and then on to FAITH training.

"Hey, Preacher!" It was the doctor I had seen earlier. "Sorry I didn't stop back at the hospital, but I knew I would be late for this meeting if I didn't keep running."

That's when the lesson hit me. As I looked around the room, now filling with busy laypeople, I recognized them as coming from all walks of life. All busy people, excited and hurrying to learn, train, and grow through the FAITH ministry. The lesson? Leaders must find and provide the way to keep busy laypeople excited and running to a ministry that will mature them in Christlikeness and equip them to win their world in their lifetime. It is incorrect and unfair to say that people are too busy or too uncommitted to pay the price and attend a church where they can be equipped to carry out Christ's Great Commission.

Many of these people were at other churches prior to joining our church, and every indication is that they would have demonstrated the same excitement and commitment in those churches if they had been challenged. Often, church leaders have the will to call for a deeper and more focused commitment from their people, but they don't have an organized approach that will bring it all together.

What makes busy laypeople turn to FAITH training? It is a ministry approach that makes sense and changes their lives and the lives of those around them. It is a common-sense procedure that is paced for a person who is involved and living a busy lifestyle. It is what I call "a training understanding" that ensures the best learning experience for busy laypeople.

Wonderful Training

FAITH Sunday School evangelism training has given me more confidence, assurance, boldness, and words to tell people about God's gift of eternal life through Jesus Christ. I always have been an active church member and involved in all areas of church work. I have taken many courses on witnessing. They in no way compare to the FAITH training in giving me a detailed gospel presentation with guidance and on-the-job training. It is more than a study course; it is a wonderful tool for equipping people to witness. The training classes have increased my scriptural knowledge and spiritual growth. My prayer life has improved to the point where it has influenced all my relationships.

JAMES H. BROWN

SENIOR ADULT 5
SUNDAY SCHOOL
TEACHER

PUBLIC SCHOOL
PRINCIPAL

THE TRAINING UNDERSTANDING

People in the church who are responsible for organizing, teaching, and training in FAITH must keep in mind that those they are equipping are busy laypeople with many things crowding their schedules. Thus, the materials are paced with appropriate built-in training helps. Class visuals and role plays are maximized. Leaders are conscious and considerate of the time and energy being invested by the attenders.

A basic responsibility of Learners is to commit to try to do the best they can, with the Lord as their primary helper. They will receive support and assistance from many FAITH helps.

This training understanding is the warm philosophy that underlies FAITH training and makes it appealing to busy laypeople. If used as prescribed, any evangelical church can use FAITH to move their fellowship to new levels of living and winning through the laypeople of their Sunday School.

JIM BISHOP

MEDIAN ADULT 3
SUNDAY SCHOOL
CLASS

CAR SALESMAN

Memory Verses

You know, 17 weeks ago if you had told me that I would be able to recite from memory nearly 10 Scripture verses, I would have thought you were crazy. Me? I took the Dale Carnegie Memory Course, but I can't remember when! I give all the credit and glory to Jesus, for He's the one who made my memorizing of verses possible.

No matter how difficult it seems, no matter how tired I am, no matter how hard Satan has worked on me, when I sit through Celebration Time and hear of people praying to receive Christ as their Savior, then I know I must keep on. Nothing is sweeter than knowing I helped the Holy Spirit win people to Christ.

Glorify God

I can't remember how many times before my Sunday School evangelism training that I had tried to share my faith but was ineffective. The memorization, guidelines, and discipline needed to complete the training successfully have been monumental in increasing not only my confidence in sharing God's love, but also God's ability to use me to glorify His name. The many times that the Lord's hand was apparent during my Team's visits gave me the confidence to say the things that I had been trained to say.

ANDY MOFFATT

YOUNG ADULT I
SUNDAY SCHOOL
CLASS

SPORTS PHYSICAL
TRAINER

Team Approach

In Sunday School evangelism training, I learned that there is a simple, straightforward way to talk about what you believe, to share the Good News of the gospel, and to show people how they can receive Jesus Christ as their personal Savior and know for certain that they have eternal life. That's exciting! I have wished that I knew how to do that most of my Christian life, but I never had the courage or took the time to learn how.

The 16-week training steps required a continued commitment from me, but it allowed me enough time to practice and learn the gospel presentation, letting my own personality come through. The Team approach and on-the-job training method let Learners see how the training approach works. It allowed us to share in our Team's witnessing effort at our own pace. I am thankful to God for FAITH and to our church leaders for providing such training for us.

ROBERT W. BURTON

MEDIAN ADULT 4
SUNDAY SCHOOL
CLASS

ENGINEER

FAITH'S ADVANCES AND ADVANTAGES

Some have said that FAITH Sunday School training is advanced Sunday School work designed for every size church now and in the 21st century. The most dynamic features are the results that come to those who participate in the FAITH ministry and those who are touched by it. There are three appealing aspects: FAITH'S ADVANCES AND ADVANTAGES, THE SUBJECTS YOU WILL STUDY, THE MATERIALS YOU WILL USE.

In regard to ADVANCES AND ADVANTAGES, the leading advantage is that Sunday School and evangelism work together effectively. Remember, evangelism training is not held during Sunday School class time on Sunday morning.

Training is provided for use of the total outline, from the opening remarks to a concluding statement. The actual gospel presentation portion also is condensed.

Preparation Section immediately connects with Sunday School and includes a Sunday School testimony by Sunday School class members, who are the visitors. This accomplishes several things and prepares for a vital closing connection with Sunday School.

An Opinion Question is used and is easier to ask by the presenter and easier to answer by the prospect than a personal question.

Gospel Presentation is done by the use of a simple acronym, FAITH. The full gospel presentation usually takes 7-8 minutes.

One Memory Device is all that is required for the trainee/beginner to learn the outline for the gospel presentation. That one memory technique captures FAITH in an unforgettable way in less than one minute!

Fewer Than Ten Bible Verses are all that are required to be memorized. Almost every Christian already knows three or four of these verses. Three additional verses are printed on the visual to help both the prospect and the presenter during the invitation

Public Confession is presented in a three-step opportunity to help the prospect to identify with, and be assimilated into the local church to grow. This is one of the most appealing parts to churches concerned with discipleship and growth. One other aspect of follow-up coupled with this closes the gap between personal professions in the home and public confessions at the church.

Video Segments are available to support FAITH training throughout the 16-week experience. They are appealing, easy to understand, and professional, assuring teams of quality material.

Computer Discs are a standard part of the training materials for FAITH. They offer state-of-the-art material for teaching each lesson. Overhead projector cels also are included.

WHAT YOU WILL STUDY

Training Clinics equip and prepare churches to effectively use FAITH Sunday School evangelism training. It is a mistake to try using FAITH approaches without the benefit of qualified clinic instruction. While this book's purpose is not to provide that training, the reader will appreciate and be encouraged by an overview of the content to be studied in FAITH.

FAITH training is devoted to helping participants learn the basic outline over a 16-week period. During that period, participants will experience:

ORIENTATION—Introduction to all materials, especially the Sunday School Evangelism concept and its implementation.

PREPARATION—Training in how to make a home visit and in preparing for the Sunday School connection and the gospel presentation.

TESTIMONIES—The development of both a Sunday School testimony and an evangelistic testimony.

PRESENTATION OVERVIEW—An overview of the FAITH Gospel Presentation.

FAITH PRESENTATION is taught with one full lesson per each of the five letters of the FAITH acronym. Appropriate Bible study and applications help participants consider implications of each letter in the word FAITH.

INVITATION—How to lead a person through prayer to receive Christ as Savior and to confess Him publicly.

A COMMITMENT BOOKLET leads a person through steps to effect a public confession of faith, a Sunday School connection, baptism, and meaningful church membership.

LIFE WITNESS EVANGELISM moves individuals to a lifestyle of witnessing in their daily lives in an effective manner.

DEALING WITH DISTRACTIONS addresses dealing with distractions and difficulties.

FAITH TRAINING ENLISTMENT is how to bring new people into the FAITH training by enlisting through the Sunday School.

STEPS TO TAKE FOR FAITH TRAINING

"Effective evangelistic churches provide good evangelism training throughout the year and teach courses at different levels," declared George Barna in the *Florida Baptist Witness*, March 7, 1996.

The steps taken to receive FAITH training and to implement an effective FAITH training ministry in your church are not as involved as they may appear below. Many of the steps are integrated into each other and flow together in a smooth and natural progression. Each step is isolated here to ensure that you have an understanding of how it all flows together and works so well. The longer you are in it, the smoother it will go.

1. READ. Completely read and then review this book. It provides an overview of the scope of FAITH. There is no other way to get acquainted with this approach and the motivation for it prior to attending a FAITH Training Clinic.

2. MISSION CONFIRMED. The Sunday School is to be confirmed by the church and its leaders as having the mission and responsibility for (1) evangelism and (2) teaching. Attending the Training Clinic will help to confirm that truth for leaders and members.

3. RECOGNIZE NEED. Leadership and church acknowledge that Sunday School members and others must be equipped to do the work of ministry, which is nurturing and evangelism, through the Sunday School.

4. UNDERSTAND FAITH. FAITH is a plan that can revolutionize Sunday School work for the 21st century.

5. ENROLL CHURCH MEMBERS. After the preparatory steps, your church should enroll as many members as possible in a Training Clinic. They are conducted at a church that is successfully doing FAITH. Training is done by qualified trainers.

6. ENROLL LEADERSHIP. Enlist the pastor and other leaders responsible for leading Sunday School and evangelism in your church to attend the Training Clinic. The section "The Pastor's Role" in Part 1 expresses how critical pastor and staff leadership is.

7. ENROLL MEMBERS. Sunday School members are the key to this ministry, so enlist as many as possible to attend the Training Clinic. Of course, you can have a successful beginning in FAITH with only a few persons attending, but it is much easier if you have more. Keep in mind that the goal is to have at least one three-person FAITH Team from each Sunday School class. There should also be FAITH Teams among Youth Sunday School. Therefore, it will be

helpful toward that goal if attenders are from different Sunday School classes. Some churches may begin with a team per department and then expand to one per class. The attenders agree to go to the Training Clinic and upon returning home, be a Team Leader on a three-person Team. The more leaders returning from the Clinic, the better your launch will be!

8. ATTEND THE CLINIC. Attending the Clinic is essential to begin and continue FAITH in your church. Don't try FAITH without Clinic preparation because you will doom and disappoint your church from the start. The Clinic will be in an approved church location where the host church is successfully implementing FAITH. The host church will have selected, qualified, and approved training teams to conduct the training.

9. LEARN. The teaching/learning approach is done in the format that is to be followed when the FAITH ministry is begun at the home church. Classroom instructions afford an overall concept and detailed training on how to conduct the FAITH ministry at home. On-the-job training brings it all together in the best possible environment.

10. RETURN HOME. When you return home, your church participants will be personally revived and will have developed a team spirit. They will possess an exciting new vision and know how their Sunday School and church can minister and grow to win the world in their lifetime!

11. USE FAITH RESOURCES. Each church is provided with resources to help begin training at home upon completion of the Training Clinic. The kit is prepared for your first 16-week STEPS, when you will train your first Sunday School group to do FAITH.

12. ENROLL LEARNERS. You are now prepared to enlist your first group of learners and begin FAITH.

13. BEGIN. You will have arranged all those enrolled into three-person Teams. Each team will consist of a Team Leader and two Learners. Each team is to have at least one man and one woman. Remember, FAITH evangelism training is not done during Sunday School class time on Sunday morning but at other times in the week.

Later, as the ministry expands, the Team will discover the need for Assistant Team Leaders and Encouragers, as mentioned in "1. Foundation—Biblical" in Part 3.

This first 16-week experience will be one of the most meaningful and memorable spiritual adventures ever for those attending.

Then, it will get better and better as the spiritual snowball starts rolling toward your goal of at least one FAITH team per Sunday School class.

14. TRAIN AND REJOICE. As you train the FAITH Teams in the way you learned at the Clinic, you will rejoice along the 16-week journey to witness participants function as predicted. This training, learning, and equipping ministry will affirm and build great Christians who will build great, growing churches that will fulfill their Great Commission through their Sunday School.

15. RECOGNIZE PARTICIPANTS. Those Sunday School members successfully completing 16 weeks of FAITH training should be significantly recognized. That is needful and helpful because: (1) they have reached a personal and collective milestone in spiritual growth and equipping, (2) recognition helps for the next enrollment effort for the following 16-week STEP, and (3) it confirms the entire church's commitment to Sunday School and FAITH.

16. ENROLL TO EXPAND. This occurs in preparation for the succeeding STEP. This is the first stage of the expansion process where the people begin to duplicate themselves and enlarge the ministry. That means more effective ministry efforts to members of Sunday School and more ministry prospects. This is the ideal time to enlist people from additional Sunday School classes in FAITH and move closer to realizing your goal of having at least one FAITH Team per Sunday School class.

17. REPEAT AND REJOICE. The above procedure is to be repeated twice a year, in the fall and the spring. This schedule allows the FAITH ministry people two well-deserved breaks. It allows them the summer free. This type of ministry cannot be sustained continually without the two STEP levels and the summer break.

These actions form a pathway to a successful FAITH ministry. Looking at them one by one reminds you of watching a youngster take first steps. Each step seems to be fearfully calculated and nervously attempted. That youngster soon is running everywhere. One day, you will see that person coaching and training someone else in his or her first steps toward running. Go for it!

GET A VISION OF "TIMOTHY TRAINING"

"The things that thou hast heard of me among many witnesses, the same commit thou to faithful men, who shall be able to teach others also. . . . Consider what I say; and the Lord give thee understanding in all things" (2 Tim. 2:2,7).

Reproductive Christians

FAITH ministry is preparing me to maximize the equipping process: equipping myself to share the gospel with others; equipping myself to disciple or "rightly divide the Word" with new believers; equipping myself to be so entrenched in the principles that my enthusiasm and eagerness will encourage others in my church and of my acquaintance to participate in reaching the world for Jesus; and equipping me to train and equip others who desire to learn how to share their faith effectively.

The magnitude of what I see in a training session enthralls and awes me—ordinary laypeople who have plowed successfully through the training, often with feelings of fear, inadequacy, doubt, and insecurities regarding their abilities. Now, they confidently are living way-of-life witnessing lives and are effectively equipping, training, and teaching others like themselves to do the same thing! What a marvelous method of fulfilling the principle of reproductive Christianity! I can visualize lines of people in heaven one day because a secretary, grocery store clerk, teacher, banker, receptionist, medical technician, telephone repairman, accountant, pest control technician, dentist, Wal-Mart greeter, housewife, or a retired man or woman right here in Daytona Beach faithfully completing this training and then expanded their vision and scope of effectiveness by continuing as a Facilitator. What a privilege, Lord, but, oh, what a responsibility! May those who come behind me in their training find me as faithful as those who've gone before. That is my prayer!

LINDA BRAGG

TEACHER
SINGLES SUNDAY
SCHOOL CLASS

SECRETARY

Those Bible verses highlight the strategic position every saved soul has as a center of influence within the learning/training plan of God. You have that strategic position, I have that strategic position, and no one can fill that God ordained spot for us. Paul says to Timothy, (1) I've learned some things. (2) Timothy, you have learned those things from me. (3) You now are to teach them to faithful believers. (4) They then should continue to teach those things to others.

THE P.I.O. LEAGUE

Guy H. King in his excellent exposition on 2 Timothy, *To My Son,* told of an encouraging decision he and some other Christians made related to 2 Timothy 2:2. King said that when he was young, a few of his committed Christian friends got together and founded a new society and called it "The P.I.O. League." They leagued themselves together to Pass It On! In spite of their shortcomings, King said, they did understand that every Christian was expected to pass on the good news.[1]

You know the old legend of the archangel's talk with the Master after His ascension back to glory. The angel had heard the story of how Jesus had lived, died, and rose. The angel's question was, "How are the people of the world to learn about all that?" The Master then replied, "I have a little group of followers there whom I have instructed to go into all the world and tell everyone." The angel then inquired, "What if those followers for some reason let you down, fail to take your command seriously, and do not tell the world? What other plan do you have?" "I have no other plan," answered the Lord.

It is through human agency that word about the Way and the Truth and the Life is to be disseminated to everyone. Humanity is God's method. An important question is "How have we been doing with our personal part in His only plan?"

We should understand how we will personally succeed in passing it on. We are to spread the good news to those with whom we have contact, but also we are to train others to do the same thing. This good news is, of course, how to be saved, but this good news goes beyond that, which is also part of our commission. FAITH is inseparably woven into the never-ending learning experience of Sunday School, where the believer regularly and systematically continues to explore the Way, the Truth, and the Life after finding personal salvation.

I do not envision the classroom teacher but the FAITH Team members doing the "Timothy Training." A Team Leader is the official trainer, but others on the team are vital to the training. By the end of STEPs, all have come together in the Follow-Learn-Teach cycle. Everyone has a thrilling taste of the "Timothy Training" blessings!

"You may not be the first link in the chain, and you may not be the last link in the chain, but you must not allow yourself to be the missing link!" I've never forgotten that admonishment I heard many years ago. Nothing could be more correct, when you look at our responsibility to pass it on as a chain. It is imperative that we not be the missing link but take our place in this chain of connections that passes it on.

Most leaders and laypeople want to have that experience in their lives and their churches, but most of the time do not. Why are there so many "missing links"? Because leaders and laypeople do not have the tools and method to bring the links together. The FAITH ministry is the structure to develop and maintain that chain.

There is the possibility of phenomenal numerical growth due to laypeople training in three-person teams. At the completion of one STEP, if the ideal occurs where each of the two who just received training become trainers of two other new people, over a time period, the result will be a large number of trained people. FAITH will continue to expand if it is done correctly.

God, through the pen of Paul, sought to have us understand that the Christian life calls for discipline in our discipleship. Christianity was never intended to be an easygoing religion, but a thoroughly vigorous affair. The Bible uses such figures as soldiers, athletes, and farmers to promulgate the Christian message. For example, the farmer is constantly toiling, up at early hours, frequently disappointed, infinitely patient, always depending upon the Lord. That depicts the Christian on mission. The Lord calls for committed workers—not shirkers.

There is no better way to ensure that you will maintain the discipline of discipleship than to be committed to the training ministry set forth by FAITH.

Would those people you listed agree that you had helped to train them? Some people can list more than 10. Most will have trouble listing 10 if they take seriously the part about "committed, organized, effective, and accountable manner."

The state of the world and the heart of our Master call for more "labourers" (Matt. 9:38). Here and now is the time and the opportunity to make a commitment to learn, train, and pass it on. "Why stand ye here all the day idle?" (Matt. 20:6).

List here 10 people whom you have trained or helped to train in a committed, organized, effective, and accountable manner to be more dedicated Great Commission Christians.

1. _____

2. _____

3. _____

4. _____

5. _____

6. _____

7. _____

8. _____

9. _____

10. _____

THE CHURCH DEVOURING MONSTER

There is a monster that lurks at the edge of the 21st century. Its tracks are plainer than ever before, and you can detect the foul scent of its presence. It is a devouring monster that has a ferocious and insatiable appetite.

While traveling across New Mexico in the summer of 1995, I saw its face more clearly than ever before. My seat was up front beside the driver in the shuttle van between Albuquerque and Santa

Fe. That pleased me because I love that scenery, and I could try to talk to the driver about Jesus.

The driver was extremely nice and talkative. We were discussing the importance of Christ in a person's life. "I've studied a lot of religions, and I've come to a conclusion," said the driver. "Religion is like a wagon wheel with its hub in the middle and spokes coming from all directions to meet at the hub. It's so logical that all religions and persuasions are like the spokes going to the same place but just from different directions. God is the hub, and all religions will eventually get you to Him." He smiled kindly and ended, "It really doesn't matter which religion, or spoke, you follow. As long as you are sincere and faithful, you'll end up happy with God at the end."

The man did not realize it, he had verbally sketched out a clear picture of "The Church Devouring Monster" that we now must battle as never before. It devours the church of Jesus Christ because it does away with Great Commission evangelism as commanded by Christ.

Likely, most evangelicals would be shocked to know how many members of their churches have bought into the same philosophy of religion described by the van driver. They have slowly but surely become as I noted earlier in "Five Frank Facts" in Part 2, "closet universalists." Such people have no interest or urgency to train, to learn, and to witness as Christ did and told us to do. They don't think that it is necessary.

This devouring monster paralyzes its prey upon an issue! Is Christianity uniquely and biblically true, or is it just another alternative to God?

After the driver's conclusion, I remembered something written by an evangelical seminary professor. I am indebted to him for his insight.

The professor pointed out that people are being required to harmonize their pluralistic approaches, including religions, because the world has become so small. Never has there been more people or a larger threat of global tragedy. Therefore, all sensitive people want to say, "Yes, whatever it takes to be at peace, let us do it, and, of course, religions should lead the way on such an issue."

Such universal pluralistic harmonizing of all religious persuasions creates an environment of world "inclusiveness." When a person maintains the position that Christianity is in fact biblically distinctive and unique, that person and that position become not popularly "inclusive" but frustratingly "exclusive" to the world.

The pressure mounts from that point on, and Christians are decried as narrow-minded, intolerant, bigoted exclusionists. J. B. Lawrence, once the Executive Director of Southern Baptist's former Home Mission Board, was ahead of his time when he said years ago:

> We who believe in Christianity as the only religion that will save the souls of men cannot place it alongside of manmade faiths. We do not deny that there are certain truths revealed in these religions; but they lack the essential elements which make the religion of Christ a redeeming and saving faith; they lack a saving knowledge of God and the power to deliver men from the guilt and punishment of sin. They do not have the Savior, the only begotten Son of God, in whom we have redemption and forgiveness of sin.
>
> The danger of tolerance is that we may so easily and completely miss the very thing which has made Christianity a power in the world. In allowing other religions a place in the field of saving truth we may easily pass to the conviction that there is little or no difference between all religions, that all of them are flickering lamps lit from a central source. That road leads straight to a colorless indifference. It has led in our modern world to a larger class of people who say, 'It doesn't matter what a man believes, so long as he believes it intensely.' People who talk like that generally believe nothing at all, or, at least, so little that they take no distinctive stand for any religion.[2]

Of course, every Christian believes in religious freedom when it comes to individuals, but there is a tragic danger in thoughtless tolerance. There are beliefs across the land today that quickly are turning our society and civilization into an ungodly wilderness wasteland.

Yes, Christianity is inclusive in that God meant *everyone* when He said "whosoever" in John 3:16. Even so, Christianity is exclusive as Jesus Christ is the only way to the Father and heaven. "I am the way, the truth, and the life: no one comes to the Father but by Me" (John 14:6). Any other worldview of Christianity is unbiblical and killing to the church of Jesus Christ and world evangelism.

Two erroneous approaches always are offered in attempts to harmonize the plurality of world religions.

One, everybody believes the same thing. Such an idea of a one-world religion is forever fostered but will never be accepted. Too many people have too many different understandings of who God is and how He reveals Himself to us.

Two, all religious persuasions go their own different ways, but all must at the end be in the same place with God. That is what the van driver concluded, and that is what the "inclusive" world pressure would have us to declare. "That view does not sound too irrational. All have their own religion. Leave them alone," some might say. If you had that thought, be careful, because your feet are already upon the slippery slope toward a view that is not consistent with God's Word.

Universalism's view denies the purpose of the incarnation, death, burial, and resurrection of Jesus Christ. That leads to disavowing the Bible, Christ, heaven, and hell. Added to that is the worst form of idolatry, that every person is released to make God in his or her own image.

What is the net result of such a redefining of the church and evangelism? Both are devoured—leaving only universalism dressed in a modern 21st- century outfit on the way to hell and taking our world with them!

The FAITH Sunday School evangelism ministry is uniquely designed to deal directly with the issue. How? By training our people to be able to know what they believe and how to articulate it. FAITH will give them confidence and will enable them to witness and win their family and acquaintances to Christ in an intelligent and effective manner.

FAITH does all that by making much of Jesus.

MAKING MUCH OF JESUS

"Neither is there salvation in any other: for there is none other name under heaven given among men, whereby we must be saved" (Acts 4:12).

The last step away from the Great Commission and world evangelism is to step away from Jesus as the only way. That is happening in the most subtle ways even within conservative evangelical circles.

I read a brochure promoting a major emphasis among evangelicals across the nation. I circled each time God was mentioned (22 times) and where Christ was mentioned (three times). The next morning, national TV news interviewed six people attending the meeting promoted in the brochure. While they mentioned God several times, Jesus' name was never spoken.

I recently was in a large group of Christian teenagers who spoke often of God but hardly at all about Jesus. "Bobby, what is wrong with talking about God?" Absolutely nothing, and you know that I believe God is God and there is none other like Him. I worship Him! But we cannot fail to let the world around us know that there is no other way to get to God except through Jesus Christ as Savior and Lord, "No other Name!" We must glorify God through His Son, Jesus, through whom our world can be won in our lifetime.

There are untold hundreds of religions, cults, and movements that talk about what they call "God," but Jesus is not the way for them. Jesus is the Christian's unique distinctive and the sole basis for the Great Commission and the salvation of this world.

Jesus' name is the master key to the powerhouse of God and answered prayer.

> John 14:13: "Whatsoever ye shall ask in my name, that will I do, that the Father may be glorified in the Son."

> John 14:14: "If ye ask any thing in my name, I will do it."

> John 15:16: "Ye have not chosen me, but I have chosen you, and ordained you, that you should go and bring fruit, and that your fruit should remain: that whatsoever ye shall ask of the Father in my name, he may give it you."

> John 16:23: "Verily, Verily, I say unto you, Whatsoever ye shall ask the Father in my name, He will give it you."

Make much of the name of Jesus, for Jesus' name is the only way to be saved. The message is plain—"Believe . . . and thou shalt be saved" (Acts 16:31). Yes, but believe in what? Believe in Christ; there is salvation in none other. "There is none other name under heaven given among men, whereby we must be saved" (Acts 4:12). The name does not save, of course, but all that name implies and stands for in regard to God, humanity, and life eternal.

Christianity is not merely a system of truth about God or a code of morality growing out of New Testament teaching. It is not simply a creed or an ethics practice. Christianity is the revelation of God in the person of His Son, Jesus. It is Christ and Christ alone who can deal with our sin and answer what a soul is reaching out for. On the cross, Jesus paid sin's penalty and redeemed us from condemnation and death unto eternal life. Christ not only cancels sin's guilt and frees us from sin's penalty, He delivers us from the power and dominion of sin in this life. Life eternal continues after this earthly existence to a glorious world without end, Amen!

The FAITH Sunday School evangelism ministry above and beyond all else is designed to MAKE MUCH OF JESUS. From the first verse to the concluding statement, those using FAITH will be trained and discipled to MAKE MUCH OF JESUS in their own life and in those with whom they speak and witness.

On the next page is your opportunity to write what your commitment will be to your journey of FAITH. Please step out into FAITH and make your commitment now.

There really is a church and evangelism devouring monster lurking at the edge of your 21st century. But, take heart because MAKING MUCH OF JESUS through FAITH is the victory!

---

[1]Guy H. King, *To My Son*. (London: Marshall, Morgan & Scott, 1944), 39.

[2]J. B. Lawrence, *Kindling for Revival Fires* (New York: Fleming H. Revell Co., 1950), 42.

My Commitment to
My Journey of FAITH

What is your commitment to do what you can

to help win our world in our lifetime?

Write it here.

PART 5

_____

_____

_____

_____

_____

_____

How Do I Get Started?

"Whoever gets into

THIS MINISTRY WILL HAVE TO GET

IN LINE BEHIND ME, BECAUSE I AND

THE STAFF INTEND TO LEAD THE WAY."

—Pastor Bobby Welch
Prior to First Training Course

A Quiet Person

My husband Floyd and I became Christians in our mid-thirties. We were in the first semester training period of Sunday School evangelism at First Baptist, Daytona Beach. I regret that we wasted years that we could have and should have been serving the Lord.

I am, by nature, a quiet person, but the Lord has blessed my ministry. One of my most thrilling experiences is when I had the joy of leading six persons to receive Christ, all at the same time, in one home.

Floyd I and have tried to make up for the years we did not know how to witness by being faithful to serve wherever the Lord would lead. We were part of the Evangelism Training Clinic from our church to go to Kiev, Ukraine. What an experience!

VIRGINIA GLADDEN

3RD GRADE
SUNDAY SCHOOL
TEACHER

PUBLIC
ELEMENTARY
SCHOOL TEACHER

THE URGENCY OF NOW

I heard of an emphasis to reach people for Jesus titled "Share Jesus Now." I liked the intent and the implication. The implication was that each person has the responsibility to "Share Jesus Now." I do. You do. "You Share Jesus Now," was the motivation.

The intent was to do it "NOW." That biblical urgency is easy to find:

> "Carry neither purse, nor scrip, nor shoes: and salute no man by the way" (Luke 10:4).
>
> "Say not ye, There are yet four months, and then cometh harvest? behold, I say unto you, Lift up your eyes, and look on the fields; for they are white already to harvest" (John 4:35).
>
> "He saith unto them, Follow me, and I will make you fishers of men. And they straightway left their nets, and followed him" (Matt. 4:19-20).

Too much of our message has lost the "now" of sharing Jesus. Too much of our music has lost the "now" of sharing Jesus. Too much of our mission has lost the "now" of sharing Jesus. Too many of our ministers have lost the "now" of sharing Jesus. Therefore, there is little wonder that too many of our church members have lost the "now" of sharing Jesus.

The last cord of evangelism today is NOW. If we do not do something now, this generation's evangelism will be like the man on the road from Jerusalem to Jericho (Luke 10:30). It will fall among robbers and be stripped of its New Testament urgency. Gone will be the heartbreak, tear shedding, the do-or-die soul winning that God told us to do when He said, "They that sow in tears shall reap in joy. He that goeth forth and weepeth, bearing precious seed, shall doubtless come again with rejoicing, bringing his sheaves with him" (Ps. 126:5-6).

We all must start living in the reality of now and witnessing in the urgency of now. Why NOW? Why must our witnessing and soul winning be done NOW? To answer that question for myself, I made a Bible list of all the reasons why I should be moved to do my witnessing NOW.

I longed for people to experience and rejoice for themselves Christ's forgiveness, peace, fellowship, friendship, support, joy, presence, and heaven. For me, personally, I discovered that beyond all those there is still one more—the most compelling reason that drives me with the urgency to go, witness, and win NOW. The motivation to win souls NOW is a clear fact of the Bible, told to us by God and taught to us by Jesus.

Evangelism Through the Sunday School: A Journey of FAITH

What makes me go more, do more, try harder, work later, get up earlier, train others, and urge more to learn how and do soul winning NOW is the reality of the torments of hell. "In hell he lift up his eyes, being in torments, and seeth Abraham afar off, and Lazarus in his bosom. And he cried and said, Father Abraham, have mercy on me, and send Lazarus, that he may dip the tip of his finger in water, and cool my tongue; for I am tormented in this flame. … For I have five brethren; that he may testify unto them lest they also come into this place of torment" (Luke 16:23-24, 28).

When I had completed my list of why I should learn how and then train others to do soul winning now, nothing came close to propelling me like the biblical fact of hell. Of course, the love of God and all the blessings of salvation are glorious reasons to win lost family members and friends. How, though, can we stand the thought of them or anyone trapped in hell?

No one wants to even think about such a possibility. I know that I do not! How horrible to imagine that people close to us would be in such a never-ending horror. It seems unthinkable that friends, family, and others actually would choose such an eternity.

"I just cannot believe that an unsaved, lost soul will go to such a place of torment as hell, for all eternity. I won't believe it. I don't believe it!" That denial is the reaction of some. Sorry to say, there are members of evangelical churches who, for all practical purposes, are "closet universalists." They live, act, and encourage those in their congregation as if there is no real hell and that all human beings will end up in heaven. As much as the human heart yearns to do away with hell, that is not possible. The Bible, Jesus, and the apostles affirm the sad fact about hell. To try and refute hell is to refuse to believe them. "Strait is the gate, and narrow is the way, which leadeth unto life, and few there be that find it" (Matt. 7:14).

Jesus did not say that "few" are on the wrong road to destruction, but "many." Why are there so many on the wrong road, headed to the horrible torments of an eternal burning hell? Regrettably, because some of the "few" on the road to heaven have lost touch with the reality of hell and have lost their urgency to win their family members and friends NOW.

The great spiritual awakening of A.D. 1734 came about largely because of the awareness of the reality of the torment of hell. Jonathan Edwards, in North Hampton, Massachusetts, preached a graphic sermon on hell to the extent that people declared that they could feel the heat and flames. The reality of hell came home, and the urgency of NOW gripped their souls. The result was an unparalleled spiritual awakening across our nation.

Books have recorded that Evangelist D. L. Moody use to tell his students heading out to be preachers, "Men, don't joke about hell—speak of hell in tears."

In addition to the truth of hell's existence and the fact of such horrible characteristics of it revealed to us from God's Word, I am aware of several real accounts that confirm the need to witness NOW.

A Buddhist acquaintance who lives in California was a young teenage Japanese boy when an atomic bomb was dropped on his home town in Japan. Fortunately, he and a friend were fishing in a valley lake hidden by mountains and miles from the city. After the explosion, they headed back toward the city and soon began to encounter people they knew—some running, some walking, some in a daze, some crawling, some moaning, some screaming, but all charred—smoking and burning. Most of them had been so quickly and badly burned that their skin seemed to be melting off their bodies. The skin from their arms had "slid" off their bones and was hanging over their hands toward the ground.

As my friend relived that boyhood day, he said, "It was like waking up in hell. It was a city of fire, torment, and screaming, with all the people burning and hopelessly and helplessly roaming about desperately searching but never finding any help or any comfort."

There have been more than a few times that the connection of that true story and the fact of a hell for all eternity has caused me to do something now to keep people I know out of hell and to get them into heaven.

It was a rainy, foggy night when a small plane crashed into the tree tops, short of the airport runway. One man was thrown from the burning plane. He was completely engulfed in flames as he ran down the hillside toward automobile headlights on a highway below. Another friend of mine, returning to the scene at daylight, retraced the burning man's desperate flight to get to help. Pieces of burning skin remained where they had been caught in the thick bushes. One spot was marked by a shoe and sock with some flesh still attached where the man attempted to rid himself of some of the fiery pain. Miraculously, the man made it to the highway and tried to stop vehicles for help. The young man who stopped to help him said that he was overwhelmed with disbelief and horror. He said that the burned man was completely charred. His hot body formed a smoking cloud around him.

The horror and torment of such a way of dying is overwhelming to me. Saddest of all thoughts about a family member or loved one going to hell is that they do not die but continue to exist in torment and flames forever.

The great preacher Hyman Appleman described hell as a world without hope. I agree.

Why anyone would follow Satan to a place without hope but a place of eternal torment and separation from God is beyond me. That is their self-chosen sentence, if Christ is not their Savior. Some skeptic may say, "You don't even know where hell is located!" Anyone who makes that accusation is mistaken. The location of hell has been exactly pinpointed. Anyone will find hell located at the end of a Christless life. Friend, you and I do not want anyone to go there in order to find it, do we? No, and that is precisely the reason we must be moved to do more witnessing NOW.

When I was just a little child.
   I heard my mother tell
Of Jesus, born in Bethlehem,
   I knew it very well.

I let it go, the years rolled on;
   My heart grew harder still.
Now I am lost in Hell today
   Because of my own stubborn will.

In Sunday School they taught me of
   A Savior from above
Who traveled all the way to Calvary
   Because of God's great love.

I neglected then to heed the call.
   I said, "I'll let it pass."
But now would give a million worlds
   For one more day in class.

One night in the revival,
 I remember it very well.
The preacher made it plain,
 'Twas either Heaven or Hell.

When they sang, "Almost Persuaded,"
 Very near I entered in,
I sold my one last chance to live,
 I died, and died in sin.

Lost forever; escaping, no, never!
 I'm lost forever and ever.
I spurned His proffered grace,
 I'll never see His face.

The saddest words of tongue or pen,
 Are these, "It might have been."
 (Author Unknown)

Even though the initial alert for us "to do something" now has been prompted by graphs and statistics, those have never been anyone's primary concern. The Christian's primary concern is and must always remain PEOPLE. Our driving urgency just must be to keep people out of hell, get them to heaven, and encourage them to glorify the Father along the way. All three of those intentions are the heartbeat of the FAITH ministry. FAITH was developed and is committed to helping Christians do their best to win their world away from hell and into heaven. Therein is the urgency of NOW!

PLEASE DON'T FORGET

As you come to the end of this book, you come to a new beginning. A new beginning in FAITH can be the most rewarding and fulfilling commitment of your Christian ministry. As you read these final pages, please don't forget several critical things.

✔ 1. Please Don't Forget—DON'T SAY NO. Don't say NO for anyone else, and don't let anyone else say NO for you as you try to win your world in your lifetime. On the day we stand in accountability before the Lord, you will not speak for anyone else, and no one will speak for you. Persons will give an account of themselves only. As surely as Jesus said, "As my Father hath sent me, even so send I

Family Changed

After praying to receive Christ through a Sunday School evangelism visit, I knew how important evangelism training was. Outside the program, I have had the opportunity to share Christ with a total stranger, two of my brothers, and a sister-in-law, and I have been able to answer many questions of my own mother. Not once did I feel that what I was sharing was unscriptural or forced. It came from the knowledge that I had gained through evangelism training. My mother was visited by one of our Sunday School evangelism teams, and she prayed to receive Christ. I look forward to sharing with my older brother and my father. Without Sunday School evangelism training, I know that I couldn't put the gospel into words in a way that they could understand and have a personal relationship with the Lord. I now feel that I can do that in my own words. The Lord has given me such a great desire to share the gospel not only with my own family, but with those around me. It is with the confidence of the Lord, not of myself, that I can do this. I am still learning, and I pray to continue to learn. This ministry has given me the witnessing tool that I need to be effective in my Christian walk. The Lord has given me everything else I need to carry out His Great Commission.

MICKEY ROBERTS

10TH GRADE
YOUTH SUNDAY
SCHOOL TEACHER

HOMEMAKER

HOWARD SIMPKINS

YOUNG ADULT I
SUNDAY SCHOOL
CLASS

U. S. NAVY

Hungry Souls

The thing that shocked me in FAITH Sunday School evangelism training was how many people we shared with who were church members but who did not know for sure whether they were going to heaven. The training has given me the desire to share my faith because of the people who are hungering for the gospel and have no one to share it with them.

you" (John 20:21). I pray each of us will hear Him say, "Well done thou good and faithful servant" (Matt. 25:21).

2. Please Don't Forget—OUR CALL TO COMMITMENT. Commitment is a call to yield our life to the will of Christ, including His great desire and commission to seek and save the lost. This is a call to step up and step out for Jesus in order to win our world.

3. Please Don't Forget—YOU'VE GOT WHAT IT TAKES, WHERE YOU ARE NOW. You have the situation, the saved people, the Savior living in them, and the Spirit of God's power. Now, you have the FAITH Sunday School evangelism ministry to help you bring it all together for the glory of God!

4. Please Don't Forget—YOU CAN BE A SOUL-WINNING DISCIPLER. Any Christian can become a soul-winning discipler right now, where the person is. There is the world that desperately needs you to do it, there is the will of God and Christ for you to do it, and there is the way, made possible through the power, Word, and Son of God to do it. You know that the Lord would never have commanded you to do anything if He did not plan to make a way for you to do it.

Please don't forget these four things as you consider taking courage and committing to running THE RISK OF EVANGELISM.

THE RISK OF EVANGELISM

"They are innovative, risk-taking, aggressive and restless." (George Barna, *Florida Baptist Witness,* March 7, 1996)

When Jesus spoke to the great multitudes, publicans, sinners, Pharisees, and scribes, each one understood and accepted His illustration of the shepherd and the sheep (Luke 15:1-17). Everyone knew that there were aspects of shepherding that were risky and dangerous. The practice was for a person to own many sheep but to hire other shepherds to watch over a certain number of sheep. Each shepherd would eventually return from the grazing pastures, sometimes far away, and account to the owner for the flock for which he was responsible. This common circumstance was the background from which the hearers listened as Jesus so powerfully illustrated His point for all of us.

"Then drew near unto him all the publicans and sinners for to hear him. And the Pharisees and scribes murmured, saying, This man receiveth sinners, and eateth with them. And he spake this parable unto them, saying, What man of you, having an hundred sheep, if he lose one of them, doth not leave the ninety and nine in the wilderness, and go after that which is lost, until he find it? And when he hath found it, he layeth it on his shoulders, rejoicing. And when he cometh home, he calleth together his friends and neighbours, saying unto them, Rejoice with me; for I have found my sheep which was lost. I say unto you, that likewise joy shall be in heaven over one sinner that repenteth, more than over ninety and nine just persons, which need no repentance" (Luke 15:1-7).

THE SHEEP

Jesus gave attention to the 100 sheep flock by dividing them into two groups. It is not complicated the way Jesus viewed this crowd of sheep. Undoubtedly, the flock was like others with thousands of different characteristics, quirks, idiosyncrasies, needs, preferences, demands, and urgencies. Beyond the sheep's individualities, Jesus saw them either safe or lost. What a critical clarification to catch through the eyes and heart of Christ! Safe or lost!

My conviction is that God sees all the people of this world the same. When God looks upon this earth, He does not primarily see city, state, county boundaries. He does not see only red, yellow, black, brown, or white. He sees only souls, and He sees only two kinds of souls—saved and lost souls. His desire is for the lost souls to be saved. His desire is for all saved souls to be attempting to get the lost souls saved through the work of the Holy Spirit. That is why I constantly remind myself that no matter where a soul is, that soul is precious and valuable in the sight of God.

Jesus made it simple when He displayed only two kinds of sheep—saved and lost.

The Ninety-Nine Sheep were the safe and saved group. The shepherd had his hands full with those that were where they should be. They were saved and safe and needed only to be cared for and kept. Jesus said, "Feed my sheep" (John 21:16); all the shepherds understood that if you have sheep they must be fed. Of course, you must find sheep before you can feed sheep.

The One Sheep was the exact opposite of the ninety-nine—the one sheep was lost and not safe. This one lost sheep, like the other ninety nine, undoubtedly had his peculiarities and individuality and surely needed to be fed, too. This one sheep had a far, far larger need in his life, however. He needed to be saved! He needed to be safe in the hands of the shepherd! Jesus said that this sheep was lost.

This one sheep was separated, afraid, aimlessly wandering, struggling to the best of his ability, unable to find the way, helpless, lonely, in perilous danger and needing immediate help! Jesus' concern was the same for this sheep as it was for all the others. Our work is to "seek and to save that which is lost."

THE SHEPHERD

As Jesus wove the occurrences, those in the crowd slowly nodded their heads affirmatively. They understand the account and agreed with the desperation of the dilemma of the sheep and the shepherd. They were aware that those of them in the crowd were to see themselves as the shepherd who was responsible for the lost sheep as well as the ninety-nine.

We, too, should be nodding our heads because we understand that we should identify ourselves as the shepherd who is responsible for the lost sheep as well as the saved and safe sheep.

It is easiest and safest to stay back with the saved and safe. The saved and safe at the church will compliment you as you devote yourself to cuddling them, caring for their wounds, combing their wool, and providing cool water for them. Truly, it is most fulfilling to the caregiving shepherd, whether pastor, staff, deacon, teacher, or member, to show love for the saved and safe. They will love, compliment, and reward on the basis of that degree of attention to their needs and concerns.

Sooner or later, however, all must stand before the owner (God) and give an account for all the sheep, including the lost. As Christ spoke that day, everyone understood that fact.

Do we understand that fact today? We are not only responsible for the crowd down at the church, we have a responsibility for the lost outside of the church. Of course, there are dangers and risks to go out in this world after the lost. There is the strategy of Satan through materialism, legal issues, "demonism," and a world of other risks with which to contend.

The love of God constrains us to take the risk of evangelism. Remember how it was when you were lost? "All we like sheep have gone astray; we have turned every one to his own way" (Isa. 53:6). "They were as sheep not having a shepherd" (Mark 6:34). Hosea 11:4 says, "I draw them with cords of a man, with bands of love." Yes, that is what causes us to go. We remember how it was when we were lost and desperate. We remember how the love of God came to us through others. That is what will give us the courage to get outside the compliments and conveniences of the church walls and run the risk to seek and save those who are lost!

The shepherds, whom Jesus loved, were committed and courageous souls. That doesn't mean that they were not scared or sometimes failed. But, they took seriously the responsibility and obligation that was commissioned and commanded to them.

When a shepherd stood before the master of the flocks, he had to have the sheep that were placed in his care or some proof of his having fought to save the sheep from the enemy. He either had the sheep or the evidence of his courage and commitment. The shepherd's only evidence usually would be wounds and scars from battling the enemy for the life of the master's sheep.

Jesus gave two views of the shepherd in John 10:11-18. Jesus compared Himself as the "good shepherd" to the "hireling" who flees because of danger. The hireling leaves the sheep to be caught by the enemy. The hireling is there only for the pay, compliments, and convenience and will not run a risk for the sheep. Jesus said that the good shepherd lays down his life for the sheep, even those outside the fold, that they may be brought into the fold.

Right now, God's Holy Spirit may be challenging your heart on this subject. You are not a hireling; you have the heart of a good shepherd but may have lost the clarity of the call of the lost. You honestly have the courage and commitment inside of you! That commitment and courage needs to come alive again, and you need a way to make it happen. The FAITH ministry can do that!

> Hast thou no scar?
> No hidden scar on foot, or side, or hand?
> I hear thee sung as mighty in the land,
> I hear them hail thy bright ascendant star,
> Hast thou no scar?
> Hast thou no wound?
> Yet I was wounded by the archers, spent,
> Leaned Me against a tree to die, and rent
> By ravening beasts that compassed me, I swooned:
> Hast thou no wound?
> No wound? No scar?
> Yet, as the Master shall the servant be,
> And pierced are the feet that follow Me;
> But thine are whole: can he have followed far
> Who has nor wound nor scar?
>
> —— Amy Carmichael[1]

Think of the privilege to know Christ in "the fellowship of his sufferings" (Phil. 3:10) as you take courage and recommit to run the risk of evangelism through FAITH.

WHAT A DAY THAT WILL BE! "Rejoice with me" (Luke 15:6). That is the result Jesus holds out to those who will run the risk of evangelism. Go after that lost sheep. It may be your own son, daughter, husband, wife, mother, father, or dearest friend. This is the resounding truth of FAITH. Loved ones will be saved!

"I say unto you, that likewise joy shall be in heaven over one sinner that repenteth, more than ninety and nine just persons, which need no repentance" (Luke 15:7).

SO THEN . . ."Let us lay aside every weight and the sin which doth so easily beset us, and let us run with patience the race that is set before us. Looking unto Jesus the author and finisher of our faith; who for the joy that was set before him endured the cross, despising the shame, and is set down at the right hand of the throne of God" (Heb. 12:1-2).

Come—Let us run! Let us run the risk of evangelism while we can so as to win our world in our lifetime!

Get Loose and Get Going

"I'M ONLY A LAYPERSON!" Have you ever heard that expression or said it? I've done both. That statement usually means, "I really cannot do as much as I would like to do because I am in this group called 'laypeople.'"

"Laity" comes from the Greek word *laos*. The word is foreign to the Bible, but it is an expression used to describe almost all of the people of the church. Those people who are not ordained as pastors and staff and do not do the work of ministry as a vocation usually are respectfully and affectionately referred to as laypeople. However, when it comes to Christ's command and commission that we are to share the gospel with the world around us, there is no difference in anyone's responsibility—pastor, staff, and laity. First Peter 2:5 says that all of us are a royal people, a peculiar crowd set apart for the work of God.

I know there are many pastors and staff who believe in the importance and significance of laypeople, but none could believe in them more than I do.

A strong emphasis of this entire book is to believe in, encourage, challenge, and equip laypeople, because they are the ones who will win this world and disciple it. They can do it too!

When John 11:38-44 is read, two pictures develop concerning a wonderful layperson named Lazarus. He was not an apostle or priest but a person who loved Jesus and lived for Him ... just a layperson.

The first picture that comes to mind is of a layperson tied and bound in a way that makes moving, doing, and going almost impossible. This layperson has most certainly been resurrected to newness of life by Jesus but has not yet been able to get loose and get going.

The second picture is the exact opposite of the first. This layperson is now loose and free to go, serve, and witness concerning the joy and power of God and his newfound life!

The big question is, "What happened to transform this bound, limited, layperson into someone who is freed and empowered to be on the loose to glorify God?" Two empowering acts are connected to cause the transformation of a layperson's life and all the world around him.

ONE, the Lord expected *other laypeople* to help get the limited Lazarus loose. In verse 44, Jesus is saying to those laypeople, "Loose him, and let him go."

Make no mistake about it, Jesus did not have to use those other laypeople. He could easily have done it Himself. Jesus could have rolled the stone away and in a moment melted those bindings from around Lazarus. But He did not. What a thrill that our Lord chose to use ordinary laypeople around Lazarus—his friends. It is a holy thing that God has allowed us to be colaborers with Him in His work (see 1 Cor. 3:9). Jesus calls upon and expects laypeople to take action to empower other laypersons.

We may be sure that those laypeople never forgot their experience in colaboring with the Lord to empower a fellow layperson. From that day forward, as Lazarus went about glorifying God in his resurrected life, those who had helped him get loose likely would say, "I was there when Lazarus got loose and got going, and I had the privilege and joy of helping him get loose from the things that held him back!"

TWO, the Lord expected *the layperson* to get going once he got loose. Lazarus was now loose, thanks to other laypeople around him, but was he going to just stand there or do something? Jesus did not tell the laypeople to move his legs for him or make him to walk. Lazarus now had the responsibility and obligation to lift his own feet and go. A farmer may pray all winter, "God, give me a good crop this year." But, that farmer will never realize that good crop until he gets up and gets going to the field and begins plowing. The Lord has a powerful, dynamic plan for every layperson, and He has an unbelievable harvest waiting for us. However, we must GET LOOSE AND GET GOING!

The FAITH ministry, as you have read, is uniquely designed and blessed to: (1) Equip laypersons to help other laypersons become empowered to be Great Commission Christians, and (2) Partner laypeople together with Sunday School to win and disciple their world in their lifetime.

The time has come for laypeople to GET LOOSE AND GET GOING—through their Sunday School. If they receive the leadership, encouragement, and training, there is no way to predict what God can do with them. Their world, and in fact the entire world, is waiting like one giant harvest field for laypeople to become equipped and then help other laypeople GET LOOSE AND GET GOING!

The FAITH Sunday School evangelism training ministry can do exactly what is needed, but we need to hurry because we must work while it is day. The night is coming when no man can work. (See John 9:4.)